UNIVERSALITY AND SELECTIVITY IN INCOME SUPPORT

Studies in Cash and Care

Editors: Sally Baldwin and Jonathan Bradshaw

Cash benefits and care services together make a fundamental contribution to human welfare. After income derived from work, they are arguably the most important determinants of living standards. Indeed, many households are almost entirely dependent on benefits and services which are socially provided. Moreover, welfare benefits and services consume the lion's share of public expenditure. The operation, impact and interaction of benefits and services is thus an important focus of research on social policy.

Policy related work in this field tends to be disseminated to small specialist audiences in the form of mimeographed research reports or working papers and perhaps later published, more briefly, in journal articles. In consequence public debate about vital social issues is sadly ill-informed. This series is designed to fill this gap by making the details of important empirically-based research more widely available.

Universality and Selectivity in Income Support

An Assessment of the Issues

SHEILA SHAVER
Social Policy Research Centre
University of New South Wales

Ashgate

Aldershot • Brookfield USA • Singapore • Sydney

Published by
Ashgate Publishing Limited
Gower House
Croft Road
Aldershot
Hants GU11 3HR
England

Ashgate Publishing Company
Old Post Road
Brookfield
Vermont 05036
USA

HD
7101
S48
.
1997

British Library Cataloging in Publication Data

Universality and selectivity in income support : an
  assessment of the issues. - (Studies in cash and care)
  1.Social security - Great Britain 2.Aged - Government
  policy - Great Britain 3. Great Britain - Social policy -
  1979-
  I.Shaver, Sheila
  361.6'1'0941

Library of Congress Catalog Card Number: 97-73612

ISBN 1 84014 137 9

Printed and bound by Athenaeum Press, Ltd.,
Gateshead, Tyne & Wear.

Contents

Figures and tables   vi

Acknowledgements   ix

1   Universality and selectivity: a review of the issues   1

2   Universality and selectivity in income support to the aged   22

3   Outcomes of universality and selectivity in the incomes of
     the aged   43

4   Universality, selectivity and public attitudes towards income
     support for the aged
     George Matheson   77

5   The Australian age pension: has targeting gone too far?   107

6   Conclusion   130

Appendix: technical information   139

References   145

Index   157

Figures and tables

Table 3.1   Coverage of income support: percentages of aged couples and single females receiving income from social transfers and means-tested transfers in six countries   48

Table 3.2   Composition of income: average share of each income component in gross income, couple and single female income units (percentages)   51

Table 3.3   Typology of universality and selectivity in income support   54

Table 3.4   Percentage of couple and single female income units below poverty lines of 40, 50 and 60 per cent of median equivalent disposable income, two equivalence adjustments   56

Figure 3.1   Percentage of couple and single female income units below poverty lines of 40, 50 and 60 per cent of median equivalent disposable income, two equivalence adjustments   57

Table 3.5   Distribution of income from social insurance transfers among quintiles of gross income for aged couples and single females   62

Table 3.6   Distribution of income from means-tested transfers among quintiles of gross income for aged couples and single females   64

Table 3.7   Distribution of income from social transfers (social
              insurance and means-tested) among quintiles of gross
              income for aged couples and single females   66

Table 3.8   Benefits and redistribution of income   68

Table 3.9   Redistribution and social expenditure on pensions   70

Table 3.10   Benefit generosity: mean social transfer income and
              mean disposable (net) income as percentage of average
              take-home pay   72

Table 4.1   Response rates and sample sizes, ISSP: 1990   83

Figure 4.1   Question 11 from International Social Survey
              Programme questionnaire, *Role of Government:* 1990   84

Figure 4.2   Question 18 from International Social Survey
              Programme questionnaire, *Role of Government:* 1990   85

Table 4.2   Public opinion on aged income support in five countries:
              1990   88

Table 4.3   Public opinion on aged income support in five countries:
              1985 and 1990   90

Table 4.4   Preference for age pension spending by approximate
              income quintile: 1990 (percentages)   93

Figure 4.3   Preferences for pension spending by employment status 96

Table 4.5   Preference for age pension spending by political
              affiliation (percentages)   98

Table 4.6   Should it be the government's responsibility to...   100

Figure 4.4   Preferences for government spending   102

Table 4.7   Percentages by party affiliation saying it should NOT
              be the responsibility of government to...   103

Figure A1.1   Percentage of males and females in age groups (persons) 140

Table A1.1   Unweighted and weighted numbers of families   141

Table A1.2:   Percentage of income unit heads aged 65+ in paid
              employment   142

Table A1.3   Mean annual social transfer income and mean
              disposable (net) income in national currencies   144

Table A1.4   Average production worker's wages   144

Acknowledgements

This project was originally conceived by Peter Saunders. My own work on it has depended a good deal on the assistance of a number of others. Marina Paxman provided research assistance over most of the life of the project. Her contributions included both literature search and review and work with the Luxembourg Income Study data sets. She in turn received assistance with the latter from Robert Urquhart, George Matheson and the staff of the Luxembourg Income Study project. Robert Urquhart completed the computational work after Marina's departure from the Centre, and Merrin Thompson gave a hand in the final stages. The research has also benefited from contributions to the e-mail list Pension Reform Interest Group (PRIG, prig@mailer.fsu.edu) and the lively discussions conducted through it.

George Matheson has taken independent responsibility for the part of the study concerned with public opinion and support for the social policy role of government. He has analysed and interpreted data from the International Social Survey Program and written the sections of the report discussing these.

Papers from this project have been presented to annual meetings of Research Committee 19, on Poverty, Social Welfare and Social Policy, of the International Sociological Association in Bielefeld, Germany in 1994 and Canberra in 1996, and to the 1995 ISA Research on Ageing Intercongress Meeting in Melbourne. A number of colleagues have commented on these papers and all or part of the present report: Bruce Bradbury, Hans Braun, Sol Encel, Ian Gough, Alois Guger, Knut Halvorsen, Barbara Hobson, Deborah Mitchell, Einar Øverbye, Joakim Palme, Stein Ringen, Peter Saunders, John Stephens, Hannu Uusitalo, Peter Whiteford, and Fiona Williams. Lynda Pawley is responsible for expert word processing in the many versions of this work and Diana Encel for assistance with editing. I am grateful to all these friends and colleagues for their help and support with this project. They bear no responsibility for its faults and limitations.

I wish to thank J. Barber, G. Moon and S. Doolan of Ageing Agendas for permission to use extracts from their consultancy report, *Targeting For Equity* (AGPS, Canberra, 1994).

1 Universality and selectivity: a review of the issues

Since the 1980s the scale of social expenditure has been in question in most advanced industrial nations. This questioning is not new, even since the 1970s, but deep-rooted changes in economies and societies have given it new force. These include slow growth, high levels of unemployment, rising levels of female labour force participation, ageing populations, high rates of marriage dissolution, and new patterns of immigration. By the 1980s, active moves were underway in many countries to restructure social policy institutions to reshape their role and restrain their growth. Reflecting these developments, the OECD (1994) has called for 'new orientations in social policy' in which government is to serve not as the 'provider of largess' but 'in partnership' with the active, self-sustaining individual. The support of ageing populations has been a primary focus of these concerns, with both the OECD and the World Bank (1994) pointing to the fiscal pressures of growing numbers of old and very old people in many countries.

One important effect of these concerns has been to renew interest in the distribution of benefit income and in particular in the role of universality and selectivity in income support measures. Both the OECD (1994, pp.11-14) and the World Bank (1994, pp.152-3) see measures to increase selectivity – narrowing rules of eligibility, targeting benefits to low income groups, flattening benefit rates, clawing back benefits through taxation – as playing an increasing role in income support in the future.

It is timely to review the issues and debates around universality and selectivity in income support. This book presents such a review, examining the claims made for selectivity in its most overt form, benefits administered through a test of means, in the light of their outcomes in the incomes of the aged. Its approach is comparative with respect to social policy choices at the level of the nation state (Lawrence, 1986). The research compares the income support systems of six countries whose income support systems give varying weight to the principles of universality and selectivity. The countries concerned are Australia, (West) Germany, Norway, Sweden, the United Kingdom and the United States.

A succession of debates

The argument about universality and selectivity in the allocation of social benefits concerns the character, distribution and limits of social rights. Of these, the social right to income support is perhaps most fundamental. The debate over universality and selectivity asks, under what terms access to income support may constitute an entitlement? In what does such an entitlement inhere? Is it need? Is it on the basis of social contribution, as in a job? Is it self help, as in having made provision for such an eventuality? Is it membership in the imagined community of the nation (Anderson, 1983)?

The argument is also about social stratification, and the distribution of economic costs and benefits among citizens and over time. Should all citizens be treated equally, or should benefits be limited to low income groups? Should the costs be borne by all, or should only those who require income protection be responsible for the burden of its cost? Should only those who have paid a share be eligible to claim benefits? Behind these questions are more far reaching ones about the appropriate pattern of redistribution for income support systems. Should the system redistribute between those who experience a particular need and those who do not? Between rich and poor? Between the present generation and the next?

There is argument, too, about the role of income support and the welfare state in the national and international economy. This concerns the scale of expenditure on income support that a given country can afford, and the slightly different question of the level that its taxpayer polity will be willing to sustain. And, finally, there is argument about the use of a test of means to measure relative need and to ration scarce resources. Is such a test stigmatising to the people it identifies as needy? Is it socially divisive? Is a fair test practicable? What kinds of resources should such a test consider? How severe should it be?

The British and American debates of the 1960s and 1970s

The arguments about universality and selectivity had perhaps their clearest expression in British debates of the late 1960s. The background was the 'peculiar consensus' (Harris, 1981, cited in Deacon and Bradshaw, 1983) surrounding the formation of the British welfare state in the immediate postwar period. Deacon and Bradshaw characterise the adoption of

2

universalist child endowment and national insurance as 'a policy which was all things to all men' (1983, p.48). The Conservative social insurance legislation of 1944 fulfilled the requirements of the Beveridge Report (Inter-departmental Committee on Social Insurance and Allied Services, 1942) in the sense that it established social insurance in which benefits represented a return for contributions, and hence were received as of right and without means test. But meanwhile the subsistence standard set for benefit levels by Beveridge had been eroded, and numbers of claimants required means-tested supplements. The social assistance of the time had dropped the hated household means test of the 1930s,[1] replacing it with a much narrower and more acceptable test (Deacon and Bradshaw, 1983, pp.39-40). The Labour Government elected in 1945 raised benefits to what it claimed represented a subsistence standard, arguing that its National Insurance Bill constituted 'virtual abolition of the means test'. However, this standard was quickly overtaken by rising prices and soon claimants were again having their benefits 'topped up' by means-tested social assistance. Deacon and Bradshaw (1983, pp.45-6) conclude that 'An enormous shift towards universalism had occurred, and the areas of means testing that remained were seen as unimportant by Labour but were sufficient to reassure the conservatives' (1983, p.48).

By the end of the 1960s the fabric of this 'peculiar consensus' was unravelling. Deacon and Bradshaw see the British debates about the relative merits of universality and selectivity as driven by the political interventions of the Institute of Economic Affairs and the Fabian Socialists and as turning on the paradox that evidence of the failure of the welfare state could be interpreted as support for both intensifying and abolishing it. Thus one side pointed to the wastefulness of paying family allowances to comfortable and even wealthy families while the other rediscovered poverty even among those receiving their full entitlements. From whichever side, the discussion raised doubts about the universalist basis of the social policy consensus. There were several strands to the debate: the role of the social services and the desirability of a return to private markets; the scope for and consequences of the introduction or extension of means testing within existing provisions; and the relationship of additional public expenditure on welfare to economic growth and the redistribution of income and wealth (Deacon and Bradshaw, 1983, pp.62-3).

The arguments of the universalists stemmed most centrally from the claim that in a society divided by class and increasingly also by race, the social inclusiveness and equality of treatment of universal entitlement to benefits contributed to social integration. Hence Townsend (1968) titled his Fabian essay, 'Does selectivity mean a nation divided?' It was argued most explicitly by Titmuss (1963, 1970), who connected it with the social legacy of shared wartime sacrifice and theorised it as 'institutionalised altruism', a 'gift relationship' of exchanges among strangers which knit society together. In contrast, the use of means tests was humiliating, requiring the applicant to declare that 'I am an unequal person' (Titmuss, 1976, p.134). A further argument appealed to social justice. Titmuss pointed out that for many recipients welfare state services were not benefits or increments to welfare at all, but rather partial compensations for the social costs and insecurities of a rapidly changing industrial society. As he put it, 'They are part of the price we pay to some people for bearing part of the costs of other people's progress' (1976, p.133).

The arguments for selective benefits were drawn from the thought of Hayek, Friedman and the Institute of Economic Affairs. They equated the principle of human freedom with economic freedom in the private market and saw social provision outside the market as a cost to the economic efficiency of the nation (Friedman, 1962; George and Wilding, 1985, pp.19-43). The proponents of selectivity maintained that universal benefits were an intrusion on the freedom of those who would have chosen to spend their money in another way, and were wasteful in giving benefits to those who did not need them. Moreover, they made taxes higher than otherwise necessary and undermined the scope for private provision through the market economy, which because it competed for capital and consumer 'dollar votes' was a more efficient way of meeting need. There was a role for public provision, but this was properly limited to areas of market failure (Friedman, 1962, pp.27-32). There was also a role for government in the support of the indigent, but only in so far as it did not undermine the scope and efficiency of the private market (Friedman, 1962, pp.33-4, 190-5; George and Wilding, 1985: Barry, 1990, pp.59-64).[2] These arguments provided an intellectual rationale for attacking the consensus surrounding universal benefits and arguing for a reversion to selective payments.

The case for universality gave higher priority to social than economic concerns, but its proponents were critical of the economic arguments made on behalf of selectivity. They pointed out that means tests typically distort economic incentives to work and to save, creating circumstances (later named 'poverty traps') in which additional effort resulted in the withdrawal of benefits. Selectivity was also wasteful in requiring expensive administrative machinery to investigate need and foster take-up. Against the claim that universal benefits were needlessly expensive, distributing scarce monies to groups who did not need them, they contended that the social cohesion secured through universality would prevent future social problems and hence save money in the long run.

4

The demonstration that the coming of the British welfare state had been accompanied by a more inequitable distribution of income than widely believed (Titmuss, 1962) and the rediscovery of poverty in its midst (Abel-Smith and Townsend, 1965) raised a different set of questions. These had to do with the role of benefits in addressing economic inequality, and were relevant only to those committed to some role for the state in moderating inequalities of income and standards of living. Those strongly committed to a market society with at most a residual welfare state saw no such role, favouring means testing simply because it minimised welfare intervention. Others, however, were attracted to selectivity because they believed this was the way to maximise benefits to the poor and redistribute income in favour of lower income groups. Appropriately devised, selective benefits might function as a form of positive discrimination. The Child Poverty Action Group, for example, campaigned for a substantial increase in family allowances, partly financed by the reduction or abolition of child tax allowances. Because the tax allowances were worth more to higher than lower income groups this would achieve a degree of selectivity while avoiding the imposition of a means test (Deacon and Bradshaw, 1983, pp.68-9).

While the British debates over universality and selectivity were often couched as all or nothing policy choices, other arguments tended to blunt the contrast. In actuality neither Hayek nor Friedman argued for conventional means-tested payments. Hayek advocated compulsory insurance (George and Wilding, 1985, p.36), and Friedman (1962, pp.191-5) a negative income tax. Labour politicians such as Crossman argued that economic circumstances and pragmatic politics set limits to the scope for universality, while academics such as Townsend and Abel-Smith pointed to the possibilities of progressive taxation and the redistribution of income and wealth for their funding (Deacon and Bradshaw, 1983, pp.70-1). Titmuss himself was never an uncompromising universalist. As he saw it,

> The challenge that faces us is not the choice between universalist and selective services. The real challenge resides in the question: what particular infrastructure of universalist services is needed in order to provide a framework of values and opportunity bases within and around which can be developed acceptable selective services provided, as social rights, on criteria of the *needs* of specific categories, groups and territorial areas and not dependent on *individual tests of means*? (Titmuss, 1976, p.122, emphasis in original).

Some of the same arguments were rehearsed in the United States, when the expansion of social programs made wholesale reform seem possible. The

5

discussion was conducted amidst recognition of poverty among the working poor as a concern of income maintenance policy and a focus on policy choice between proposals for a negative income tax or a family allowance. Some of the character of the American debates of the 1970s can be seen in a conference of leading social scientists convened by the University of Wisconsin Institute for Research on Poverty to discuss the role of means testing in income maintenance policy in 1979 (Garfinkel, 1982).

These discussions drew on British as well as American debates and were conducted in much the same terms, setting trade-offs between cost and efficiency of social programs against problems of stigma and social division. However, the American discussions took place in, and to some extent challenged, a consensus of academic and policy opinion in that country favouring income-tested programs over those not requiring a test (Garfinkel, 1982, pp.2-3). This difference in context made aspects of the debate differently salient. For example, while British debates emphasised problems in the take-up of means-tested benefits, American discussions highlighted their implications for economic incentives (see Garfinkel, 1982). Concerns were raised about the sometimes perverse effects of selectivity on incentives to earn, and about its potential to encourage fraud (Glazer, 1988, p.86).

While British argument had contrasted the economic and social dimensions of universality and selectivity, the American debates gave new prominence to the political dimension. In particular, questions were raised about the consequences of universal and selective benefits for voter and taxpayer support for social expenditure. In its sharpest form, the argument suggested there might be a trade-off between the target efficiency of income-tested benefits and their electoral popularity. Because affluent beneficiaries were likely to exert greater political influence than poor beneficiaries, an increase in the proportion of affluent beneficiaries would generate political support for spending, and hence favour a higher average benefit than would otherwise be the case. It might thus be to the advantage of the poor to share their benefits with the non-poor. This might, however, not always be the case, as the high universal benefits enjoyed by some might attract the political hostility of taxpayer groups excluded from benefits because they were, for example not old or the parents of dependent children (Jencks, 1982, pp.93-5).

The British and American debates of the 1960s and early 1970s argued the relative merits of universality and selectivity within comparatively narrow confines. Sharing the policy legacy of English liberalism and the poor law, debates in both countries posed the issues in stark terms, invoking images of policy choices as between capitalism and socialism, freedom and totalitarianism. The terms of these debates obscured some issues in the contrast of universality and selectivity important in other countries. One such question is the relative merits of benefits based on residence and citizenship as compared with those framed as insurance. Another concerns benefit levels and the scope and effects of inequalities in the incomes of recipients. These issues have figured more strongly in recent comparative study of welfare state development drawing on T.H. Marshall's (1963) portrayal of welfare state entitlements as representing a twentieth century development of citizenship.

Citizenship and universality

Marshall's thesis is well known. In his seminal essay 'Citizenship and social class' (1963), he argued that the entitlements of the welfare state mark the development of a new dimension of citizenship, 'social rights' created on the basis of, but also in problematic tension with, the civil and political rights of citizenship. Drawing on the British example, Marshall regarded the social rights of citizenship as establishing a form of social equality which had proved compatible with the economic inequalities of capitalist society. These ideas have provided a starting point for historical and theoretical discussion of the development of the western welfare state and in particular for understanding variations in the form its development has taken in the countries of Europe, America and Australasia.

The meaning of social citizenship in the welfare state has been variously understood. The least demanding interpretation of citizenship associates it with the replacement of poor laws and the institutions of the workhouse, outdoor relief and discretionary charity by the types of social provision which began to be instituted at the end of the nineteenth century. These developments did not mark the first emergence of the notion of welfare as a right, which had rather been intrinsic to feudal relations of mutual service and obligation. It is commonly pointed out that in England the replacement of the Speenhamland system was undertaken precisely in order to curtail such customary rights (Esping-Andersen, 1990, p.36). The distinctiveness of the systems of means-tested social assistance introduced in some countries and of social insurance in others lies in their supplanting punitive conditions for poor relief by forms of social provision which did not entail the loss of civil or political rights of citizenship (Marshall, 1963; Orloff, 1993, p.10).

This interpretation defines the basic threshold of social rights of citizenship. The emergence of these early forms of social provision saw a change in the relation between welfare claimancy and civil status. Previously a claim to assistance meant the loss of civil and political rights.

7

Henceforth a claim was consistent with, and indeed confirmed, social status as a member of the community. This is the bedrock of equality: these were new forms of social provision, and they represented some degree of economic security and social legitimacy for age groups who had lacked both.

Social citizenship is more usually identified with Marshall's own historical moment in the establishment of the postwar welfare state. The initial forms of social citizenship manifested in means-tested social assistance and early versions of social insurance were rarely intended as providing full subsistence, but rather presumed access to other resources through employment, kin relations or community. For Marshall, social citizenship entailed the guarantee, as of right, of a minimum standard of wellbeing necessary to support full membership of a community (Barbalet, 1988, p.5). The importance of this minimum is twofold, for it represents not only the insulation of the individual against the worst adversities of the market and capitalist economy but also an affirmation, in material form, of the value of the individual as a participant in society. Citizenship is a status of equality with other members of the community in honour and dignity. This status is bestowed by the welfare state only when it gives access to a material minimum, and does so by right of community membership. It is this status of honour and dignity as a human being, expressed in the right to a minimum quantum of economic resources, which provides the foundation for full participation in civil society and political process.

The identification of citizenship with the postwar development of the welfare state reflects an anglocentric bias in the interpretation of welfare history. Most advanced industrial nations, including the UK, introduced old age pensions before the war. There are, nevertheless, important differences between modern and earlier social provision, though these differences are less marked in Germany than elsewhere. These differences lie in the fuller development of social provision with respect to both state responsibility for ensuring a minimum material standard and for its availability on a basis of right. Bureaucratic and professional development replaced moralistic and discretionary modes of access by codified rules of eligibility and entitlement. The community was more fully defined by social security systems encompassing a large share of the population in the circulation of benefits and revenues. Citizenship in this sense has almost always been national in scope, and benefits individually determined.

Still other interpretations have sought to extend the idea of citizenship beyond Marshall's social minimum, stretching its horizons to allow broader aspirations toward social and economic equality. A gesture of this kind is implicit in Titmuss' (1974) famous 'models of social policy', characterising the underlying values of social policy as residual, industrial/achievement, and institutional/redistributive in nature. The residual model drew its essence from early social assistance, and the industrial/achievement one from the wage-related social insurance of the postwar period. The institutional/redistributive model attempted to spell out an ideal vision in which a broad range of institutions enabled the members of its community to share in both giving and receiving. Always difficult to pin down, its imagination drew on an idealised Scandinavia. The vision of citizenship implied in the institutional model of social policy puts very great weight on the importance of dignity in the meeting of human need, which Titmuss saw as most fully ensured when the use of the social services was a general condition of society. The place of a guaranteed minimum standard of wellbeing is here taken by the more abstract, but potentially more far-reaching, notion of the redistributive welfare state. In its redistributive role the welfare state not only ensures that all citizens have access to the resources to meet their needs but also provides the institutional framework within which all are givers as well as receivers. Mishra (1981, p.14) has signalled its broader implications in his observation that the residual and institutional models become much clearer - though Titmuss himself might not have agreed - if one imagines a third possibility in 'structuralist' social policy, which would recognise the limitations on social policy inherent in capitalist society.

Myles' (1989, pp.28-9) interpretation of the 'citizens' wage' is analytic, designed to capture the ambiguous, hybrid character of public old age pensions in capitalist society. He portrays old age pensions as compounding contradictory elements of the liberal ideology of wage justice, in which the pension is understood as deferred income from employment and therefore properly unequal in value, and democratic values of social equality, in which the pension incorporates a share of the social product over and above the wage and is appropriately downwardly redistributive. Myles' interpretation is founded on Marshall's, but gives the notion of citizenship an inflection of extractive social justice. The material element is more important than the symbolic in Myles' analysis, though ideas about equality and the social meaning of entitlement figure in the political economy of pension development.

Finally, Esping-Andersen and the power resources school more generally identify citizenship with the (limited) emancipatory potential of the welfare state to 'decommodify' human life (see also Offe, 1984; Korpi, 1983; Palme, 1990b). Esping-Andersen (1990, pp.21-6) further elaborates the concept of citizenship, developing it in two dimensions. The first concerns the quality of social rights and the rules and conditions governing them:

9

social rights must be secure, adequate in material substance, and granted on terms which dissociate benefit entitlements from market performance. But, Esping-Andersen notes, social rights carry with them economic and social statuses, and so also serve to place their bearer in a given social stratification modifying, or perhaps supplanting, class position. The social rights constructed by the welfare state thus entail an active ordering of social relations.

Esping-Andersen reserves the badge of citizenship for frameworks of social rights which establish a degree of insulation of the wage worker from abject dependence on the labour market. This is because together the two dimensions of citizenship shape the capacity of the working class to pursue its political interests through wider alliances with adjacent groups. Baldwin (1990) develops much the same argument in the more generalised terms of social insurance and the common interests of the 'risk groups' it defines. He points also to the reciprocal relation between state and citizenship - that the shape of social rights comes to reflect the alliances of the 'risk groups', and in particular the interests of the middle class groups occupying pivotal positions in the politics of alliance.

Citizenship has often been directly and literally equated with universality in the provision of benefits. This has been most marked in the areas of health services and income support, where it has been most commonly argued with respect to child benefits and old age pensions. This equation of citizenship with universality rests largely on interpretations of what constitutes a meaningful basis of right in access to the social entitlements of the welfare state. As we shall see, however, this is not so straightforward as it at first appears.

Ware and Goodin (1990, pp.5-9) have slightly reformulated Titmuss' three models of social policy referred to above, clarifying the principle of eligibility which underlies each. These correspond reasonably closely to the three basic principles underlying social security systems, or parts of systems, in modern welfare states. Their *residualist (or needs-based)* model operates on the principle that everyone is potentially eligible for the assistance necessary to reach a minimum standard, but that such assistance is actually provided only to those who experience actual need, and who satisfy a test that such need is genuine. In the case of financial assistance this normally entails a means test of some kind. The *insurance (or contributions-based)* model parallels Titmuss' industrial achievement model and is organised on the principle that eligibility for assistance should depend on a history of past 'contributions' building interests in a fund, and that the level of benefits be linked to that of contributions. The *social citizenship (or rights-based)* model has parallels with Titmuss' institutional redistributive model of social policy, but in Ware and Goodin's schema is unambiguously identified with membership in society through residence or legal status, and with equal eligibility, unqualified by either a test of means or the requirement of past contributions.

Each of these models can be seen as representing universality in some form or other. In principle the protection given by needs-based assistance is available to all, though the actual receipt of assistance is limited to those who fall below the minimum standard. Contributions-based assistance is universal in the sense that it encompasses the full population of workers and their dependants in a single framework of provision. This has been called the 'citizen-worker' model of welfare provision (Hernes, 1987).

But it is the third model of rights-based provision which is most widely identified with universality. Palme (1990a, p.106) refers to it as the most unambiguous condition for acquiring a right to a pension. Given its direct and unmediated identification of eligibility with community membership as resident or legal citizen, universality represents the apparently natural expression in social policy of the equality of liberal democracy.

In his reading of Marshall, Barbalet understands citizenship as necessarily requiring universality. This is because citizenship is inherently and essentially two dimensional, requiring not only that all members of society share in access to economic subsistence but also that they share in the common experience of government administration.

While earlier forms of class abatement alleviated the condition of poverty they tended to reinforce the class divisions between those to whom the services were provided and those who did not require them. The universalisation of social services as a right of citizenship, on the other hand, has meant that the vast majority of citizens are subject to the same process through which the services are provided and receive essentially the same benefit. This common experience reduces the social distance between citizens (Barbalet, 1988, pp.50-1).

However, this equation of citizenship with universality can be questioned. Two particularly important objections have been raised. The first is that there is a fundamental contradiction in the notion of citizenship between its nature as a universal status and its identification as a bundle of universal social rights. The second is that universality itself is immaterial to the goals of citizenship if these are taken to be substantive equality as an outcome of welfare state provision, either as the achievement of a minimum standard of wellbeing or as the enhancement of equality through more all-embracing patterns of redistribution.

Barbalet (1988, pp.67-72) finds a contradiction between the universality of citizenship and the particularity of the needs and circumstances of

11

individual citizens. In parallel with civil and political rights, the social dimension of citizenship is a condition of participation in a common national community. The universality of citizenship is thus abstract, by its very nature formally equal for all members of the nation community. In contrast, social rights are substantive, consisting of material provisions subject to specified qualifying conditions and meeting individually different needs. In this sense social rights cannot be said to be the same, hence universal, for all citizens. Barbalet overstates this contrast; like social rights, civil and political rights are also institutionalised in universal forms yet in practice have unequal value to different individuals and the members of different social groups. Nevertheless a contradiction remains between the status content of citizenship and the substantive content of social rights.

In the arguments of Esping-Andersen (1990) and Baldwin (1990) the connection between citizenship and universality is strategic. Esping-Andersen's is the more general theory, and is centrally concerned with accounting for diversity in the institutional structures of advanced capitalist welfare states. He sees universality in benefit entitlement and financing as one of the defining characteristics of the social democratic welfare state type. Baldwin focuses on the redistributive interests inherent in social insurance and the play of politics among the 'risk groups' defined in contending social policy proposals. He too identifies universality with the Scandinavian welfare states, and to a lesser degree also with Britain. Both authors identify universality with social solidarity and its strategic importance in forging political alliances among interest groups and social classes in the development of the welfare state. In forgoing the immediate redistributive gains of benefits limited to their own class or risk group, universalist social policy enabled social democratic parties to forge coalitions of workers with farmers and middle class groups. As Baldwin (1990, p.112) writes, 'Universality seemed to have been a fruit of the left's ability to translate claims put forth by the unfortunate into common interests shared by a majority of society.' As this quotation implies, Baldwin gives greater credit to the the middle classes for the strategy of solidarity than Esping-Andersen.

The contradiction between symbolic and substantive equality is played out in the politics of old age pensions in various welfare states. Arguments about the merits of their various forms, as in the models proposed by Titmuss and by Ware and Goodin above, turn on the relationships between universality or selectivity of income support and appropriate standards of equality among citizens. The redistributive virtues of means-tested social assistance are said to be secured at the cost of claimants' dignity, and hence inconsistent with the equality of status inherent in citizenship. Social insurance, while encompassing workers of all classes, transforms the inequalities of the capitalist labour market into substantive inequalities in social provision. Universal, flat rate provision treats all citizens equally, but by virtue of that fact does little to redress wider inequalities.[3] Thus all three frameworks entail a contradiction in some form between the basis of right and the adequacy of support.

Universality, selectivity and welfare state restructuring

Side by side with the discussion about citizenship and the welfare state, the issues raised in the British and American debates were rehearsed again in the 1980s. This time the debate concerned the relative virtues of universality and selectivity in the adaptation of the welfare state to a changing socioeconomic environment. While the issues themselves had changed little, the emphasis placed on them has been altered by the changed climate.

These discussions came in the wake of what was called for a time the 'crisis of the welfare state', and later understood as its restructuring in adaptation to global changes in capitalist societies and economies. Profound changes began to be apparent in the 1970s, raising fundamental questions about the ability of governments and the welfare state to sustain economic growth with full employment and modest redistribution indefinitely. With hindsight, the emergence of simultaneously rising rates of unemployment and inflation can be seen as marking the end of the postwar era and the commencement of a new historical period of institutional adaptation. The perception of change in the terms of crisis also owed something to the apocalyptic qualities of radical social and political analysis of the 1970s, particularly the social policy arguments drawn from marxism on one side and the new right on the other. As the 1980s wore on, however, theories of crisis gave way to discourses of welfare state restructuring, weakening the force of the 'grand narratives' of capitalism and socialism (Pierson, 1991, p.141; Taylor-Gooby, 1991; Klein, 1993). By the late 1980s the overtones of crisis had been replaced by staid assumptions of incrementalism and a new recognition of the importance of institutional structure across the social sciences.

These changes have taken varying form in particular countries, but generally have entailed conjunctions of slowed economic growth with growing claims on welfare expenditure. The competitive pressures of an increasingly international economy and political resistance to taxation have made it difficult for governments to raise revenues for social purposes. At the same time, pressures on social expenditure stem not only from higher rates of unemployment but also from demographic ageing of the population,

13

stresses on families associated with increasing numbers of both dual earner and single parent households, and technological developments requiring extended workforce education and training. Welfare states are being restructured to adapt to these and other changes. According to Friedmann, while there has been little change in the various goals of welfare states there have been changes in the relative emphases given to them, and with these changes in the policy mechanisms employed to achieve them. These have variously included increasing targeting of benefits, but also decentralisation of benefit administration, policy shifts favouring private sector provision, and reduction in the real value of benefits (Friedmann, 1987, pp.284-7; see also Morris, 1988).

While the arguments of the 1960s and 1970s about universality and selectivity were shaped by the portrayal of selectivity as a vestige of the past and the poor law, those of the 1980s and 1990s have been driven by the case to be made for it in the constrained circumstances of the future. In the process, the debates give greater prominence to the economic and less to the social dimensions of the contrast between universality and selectivity than the discussions of the earlier period. Contemporary arguments in favour of selective payments stress their capacity to direct expenditure to those with greatest need, and hence to operate with comparatively low levels of social expenditure and minimal disturbance of the processes of the market economy.

These arguments have been put particularly forcefully in Australia, where income support is almost wholly selective. Australians have long defended the selectivist approach as ensuring a more effective redistribution of resources to those in greatest need. The poverty alleviation objective is thereby achieved at minimum cost to the budget and, by implication, to taxpayers generally. Australia may well spend less on social security transfers than other OECD countries, but because of the selectivist nature of the Australian system a greater proportion of what is spent is devoted to those most in need (Henderson, 1977). In a situation where overall fiscal restraint places constraints on the growth of social expenditure, the arguments for increased selectivity seem even more compelling. Saunders (1994, p.45) states the conventional wisdom as holding that the redistributive impact of a given volume of expenditure will be greater the more effectively benefits are targeted on those in greatest need. Selective or targeted benefits thus permit 'restraint with equity' to be achieved in practice.

Questioning this conventional wisdom, Saunders (1994, p.45) contends that the argument on selectivity is predicated on the assumption that the volume of funds available for redistribution depends on the willingness of taxpayers to finance a social role for government. An undue emphasis on targeting may in fact serve to undermine public support for social security, reducing the level of social security expenditure. It is recognised that selectivist approaches are likely to encounter problems with respect to incentives to work or to save, and may create poverty traps, and proponents of greater universalism stress the role universal payments can play in maintaining incentives to work.[4] The symbolic importance of universal payments in affirming equality and citizenship is argued principally by proponents of Basic Income (Whiteford, Bradbury and Saunders, 1989; Probert, 1995; Cappo and Cass, 1994).

Australian arguments have given comparatively little weight to issues of stigma and social division, and it is true that these issues have not featured prominently in the history of Australian pension development (Shaver, 1991). They have also been less concerned with issues of take-up than have arguments in the UK (Saunders, 1991, p.311; Deacon and Bradshaw, 1983, pp.122-49). Importantly, Australian pensions and benefits differ sharply from their selective equivalents in most other countries in the generosity of the means tests applied to determine benefit entitlement, making the receipt of a pension or benefit a comparatively common social experience in that country (Shaver, 1991).[5]

From the 1980s provisions for income support in old age, everywhere a major source of public social welfare expenditure, have come under increasing scrutiny (Friedmann, 1987, p.247). Nevertheless the aged have generally fared better than able-bodied workers (Morris, 1988, p.12). According to Morris (1988, pp.22-5), there is widespread acceptance of the proposition that public benefits should be more closely targeted upon those who need them most. He reviewed nine countries: Britain, Sweden, West Germany, Austria, Italy, Yugoslavia, Israel, Japan and the United States. He suggests that a marginal movement towards means testing was underway in the 1980s, often under the cloak of social insurance. While only marginal, this movement was proving sufficient to damp further advances in universal benefits. In a more recent review of trends in pension reform in the OECD countries since the early 1980s, Myles and Quadagno (1997) argue that while there has been a common pattern of constraint it has taken different form in the 'Beveridge' and 'Bismarck' countries. The former, relying on basic security programs as the major pension vehicle, have adopted a tax/transfer model of reform in which benefits are increasingly being means tested and the link between contributions and benefits weakened. The latter, relying mainly on earnings-related social insurance programs, have seen the link between contributions and benefits tightened. Taylor-Gooby, George and Bonoli (1995) report there being strong support for targeting among policy makers in six European countries, though principally for its application to family benefits. There was support for increased targeting of retirement provisions in the two countries (Denmark and the UK) having flat rate benefits.

In actuality universal and selective income support instruments have been differently developed from country to country, and moreover, the income support systems of most countries combine elements of several kinds. Some writers now argue that outcomes are relatively independent of instruments, and that it is only outcomes that matter. Welfare states, they argue, should be compared in terms of their performances, measured in the achievement of low levels of poverty and moderation of income inequality.

Ringen (1987, pp.7-14), for example, considers that the goal of equality can be given a weak or a strong interpretation in the politics of welfare state development. A weak interpretation aims at a guaranteed minimum standard for all members of society, while a strong formulation refers further to the entire structure of inequality. 'In the first case, the ambition is to eliminate destitution and individual misery, in the second case to eliminate, in addition, societal cleavages which might cause conflict and tension in society' (Ringen, 1987, p.7). He identifies this latter goal with citizenship, and argues that the size of the welfare state is a more meaningful indicator than is the use of universality or selectivity in its programs. This point of view has, however, been trenchantly criticised (Esping-Andersen, 1990, pp.19-21; Castles, 1994).

Mitchell (1991) examined the tax and transfer systems of ten welfare states with respect to their efficiency and effectiveness in reducing income poverty and inequality. Her data relate to the period around 1980. She dismisses the conventional wisdom about the relative merits of universality and selectivity in benefit administration as unfounded. On the basis of her research there is no clear and necessary association between the universality or selectivity of benefits and either effectiveness or efficiency.

It may, indeed, be true that minimum material standards can be assured, and effective redistribution of income achieved, through a wide variety of transfer and taxation instruments. Nevertheless, it is difficult to believe that the institutional contours of the welfare state are irrelevant, for they give the provision of welfare income its particular and variable social meaning. These contours are, in fact, the stuff of welfare politics, for they have embodied in them ideas about individual behaviour, social justice, and the collective interests of social groups. Reference has already been made to the social contours of welfare state benefits in shaping political alliances (Esping-Andersen, 1990; Baldwin, 1990) and the willingness of taxpayers to fund high levels of social expenditure (Saunders, 1994, p.45). They also affect the social experience of individual recipients, including that of stigma, status honour and social justice. It has also been argued that institutions have especial importance in welfare state politics of retrenchment (Pierson, 1994). The approach of the present study is to draw its hypotheses from the arguments about the role of institutional arrangements, but to treat their effects in terms of outcomes as a matter of empirical investigation.

The issue of universality and selectivity in the instruments of public income support is part of a broader set of questions about the packaging of retirement income and the policy choices governing it. This entails wider comparative study elucidating the relative roles of income support, private pensions, private financial investments, and non-monetary returns such as from owner occupied housing in the income packages of the aged under different policy conditions. The key questions here concern the effect of public provision on wage and salary incomes, on savings and investment behaviour, and on the political behaviour of voters and parties. It might be asked, for example, whether universality or selectivity in public income support is more encouraging of private pension provision. The role of private saving through housing is also important. It has been suggested that policies favouring owner occupied housing alter the balance of incentives encoded in income support policy, and that selective income support arrangements may encourage saving through home ownership (Castles, 1996). The present research does not address this broader set of questions, but is confined to the narrower focus of universality and selectivity in state income support.

The focus of the study

The present study aims to weigh the substance of some of the claims made on behalf of universality and selectivity by comparing the outcomes of differing kinds of income support system in the incomes of aged people. Its approach is quantitative and comparative, exploring similarities and differences in the levels and distributions of income in countries whose arrangements give different weight to the principles. of universality and selectivity. From the succession of debates about the relative merits of universality and selectivity in income support, a series of questions have been identified as important in the current context of welfare state development and social policy.

1   *What do universality and selectivity mean in practice in the income support systems of various countries?* Discussions of universality and

selectivity have generally been conducted as a simple, one dimensional contrast, but in actuality income support systems are far more complex. While selectivity can be unambiguously identified with means-tested benefit allocation,[6] universality is variously associated with eligibility for benefits on the basis of social insurance and social citizenship. The income support systems of most countries combine at least two and often three of these elements. An associated question concerns the relative importance of universal and selective benefits in gross income and the relationship between benefit and non-benefit income associated with different types of income support arrangement.

2   *Are selective income support arrangements more effective than universal ones in ensuring low levels of poverty?* The central claim made on behalf of selective benefits is that they ensure that resources are directed to those who need them most. The research is accordingly concerned with comparisons of the relative size of the group below various poverty standards in countries whose income support arrangements give different weight to universality and selectivity in benefit allocation.

3   *Is it true that selective income support arrangements concentrate social expenditure on those with least other income, and that in doing so achieve greater redistribution in favour of low income group than universal arrangements?* This question allows fuller examination of the claim that selectivity is more effective than universality in directing benefits to those who need them most, and that the apparent residualism of selectivity is belied in the achievement of greater redistribution in favour of low income groups. Selective income support arrangements typically involve lower levels of social expenditure than universal systems, hence an important associated question is, *do selective income support arrangements achieve a given level of redistribution of income more efficiently than universal ones?*

4   *Is it the case that benefit levels are less generous under selective than universal income support arrangements?* Poverty alleviation depends not only on directing benefits to those who need them but on providing benefit at high enough level to bring income to an adequate standard. It is often said that benefits to the poor are poor benefits, and that in concentrating benefits on low income groups selective benefits fail to secure the political support of middle income taxpayers for social expenditure.

18

5 *Does the picture presented in surveys of political opinion suggest that there are lower levels of public support for social policy expenditure in countries with selective than universal income support arrangements?* This is a more direct way of considering the claim that universality and selectivity in the construction of benefit systems feed back into the political system and political support for the activities of the welfare state.

6 *Can the pursuit of effectiveness and efficiency through selectivity become counterproductive?* Given its central reliance on means-tested benefits, Australian income support provides a useful case study of the possibility that selectivity and targeting can be taken too far. Concerns arise with respect to both economic effects such as distortion of incentives to work and save and social effects such as stigma, loss of social cohesion and declining levels of benefit take-up.

These questions situate the comparison of universality and selectivity on the ground of selectivity. Another study might have given greater weight, and accorded greater scrutiny, to claims made on behalf of universality such as the fostering of social cohesion and the social values of citizenship. As noted above, these contentions are critical to the case for the social policy proposals aimed at breaking the nexus between a minimum standard of income and access to employment (Pixley, 1993, pp.87-124). This study has taken its point of departure from contemporary policy developments now underway in the process of welfare state restructuring in the context of fiscal constraint. These arguments bear directly on contemporary policy development in many countries at the present time.

The contrast between universality and selectivity has been framed in a variety of ways. Some writers (Myles and Quadagno, 1997) distinguish between the Bismarck and Beveridge traditions of wage-related and flat rate provision, both of which are typically underpinned by social assistance. The 'power resources' school combines the contrast between selective or means-tested and universal payments on the basis of citizenship or residence with a second dimension referring to the capacity of the benefit system to displace the forces of the private market. This approach lies behind Esping-Andersen's (1990) typology of 'liberal', 'corporatist' and 'social democratic' welfare states. Korpi and Palme (1996) include it in a wider typology of social insurance institutions ranging from 'targeted' income support systems such as the Australian to 'encompassing' arrangements of the kind found in Scandinavia. These typologies aim to capture both the political and the economic dimensions of pension systems. The present research is more narrowly concerned with the distributive character of universal and selective instruments, for which a simpler approach is appropriate. This approach gives less weight to the distinction between citizenship-based and wage-related provisions than to the distinction between benefits which are targeted on low income groups and those provided on an inclusive basis, whether or not this is income-related.

Selectivity itself can be understood in a number of ways, but for the purposes of the present inquiry has been identified with the allocation of benefits on the basis of a test of means. As often observed (Ringen, 1987; Mitchell, 1991; Saunders, 1994), the relation of benefit income to need can be secured through a great variety of mechanisms, including categorical rules of eligibility and tax clawbacks as well as means testing. Means-tested allocation is, however, the most overt and direct form of selectivity in income support. It has attracted the greatest controversy (Townsend, 1968, pp.3-4), and its use has been growing in recent years.

In principle, the debates about the relative virtues of universality and selectivity apply across most of the broad range of welfare state programs. Lively versions of these arguments are current, for example, in the fields of health and education. The focus of the present study is on income support, as an area where the contrast between universality and selectivity can be drawn particularly sharply and where data are available for comparative, quantitative research.

Similarly, the issues associated with policy choice between universality and selectivity arise across the range of income support programs. This study is limited, however, to income support programs for the aged. Universality, selectivity, and welfare state forms more generally find their strongest expression in old age pension systems. These tend to be the oldest areas of modern welfare state provision, and to account for the largest share of their resources. As Guillemard (1983, p.3) puts it, 'The welfare state is first of all a welfare state for the elderly'. Moreover old age has long been identified as one of the two life cycle periods when the risk of poverty is greatest (Hedstrom and Ringen, 1990, p.77). This risk has been addressed by the welfare state in varying ways and to varying degree. Old age pensions thus provide an appropriate area of focus for an examination of the claims made on behalf of various forms of income support provision.

The chapters to follow address the six questions listed above through comparative study of income support to the aged in six countries. The next chapter gives an account of the development of universal and selective approaches to welfare state provision and describes the systems of aged income support operating in the six countries in the mid 1980s. Chapter 3 presents an analysis of data from the Luxembourg Income Study as they bear on questions (1) to (4). This discussion covers the practical expression of universality and selectivity in the income support systems of these countries, their effectiveness in alleviating poverty among the aged, the extent to which they redistribute income among the aged, and the relative generosity of the benefits they provide. Chapter 4, by George Matheson, is concerned with question (5), using public opinion data from the International Social Survey Program to compare attitudes to the role of government and support for social expenditure in five of the six countries. Chapter 5 focuses on Australia and the practical problems of administering means-tested income support, asking about the costs of selectivity in economic disincentives and loss of social cohesion. The final chapter brings the findings of the study together.

Notes

1   This test regarded the resources of each member of the household as being available to meet the needs of the claimant, whether or not they were related. It thus forced the unemployed to be supported by parents, children, siblings or even unrelated adults living in the same household (Deacon and Bradshaw, 1983, pp.16-17).

2   Friedman also accepted the necessity of intervention in the lives of those intellectually incapable of the responsibilities of the free individual (Friedman, 1962, pp.33-4).

3   Le Grand (1982) argues that such benefits favour the middle classes, who are able to make more advantageous use of them. This is likely to be a less significant factor in the case of income support than of access to professional services such as health care and education.

4   A similar argument is made by British proponents of a Social Dividend (Wilson and Wilson, 1991, p.28).

5   Kamerman and Kahn (1987) have made a similar case with respect to means-tested benefits to families with children in the United States. They argue for the extension of means-tested benefits within a larger framework of entitlements which though universal are subject to income taxation.

6   Selectivity can, however, also be achieved by other means, the most important being the rules used to categorise eligibility and clawbacks through taxation.

2 Universality and selectivity in income support to the aged

Peter Flora (1986, p. xv) suggests that the welfare state represents a 'completion' of development of the nation state, in that the social rights which it confers are integral to citizenship and the legitimacy of the liberal democratic state. Such completion is, however, less than full. Flora notes that few social rights are citizen rights in the strict sense, for they are more commonly attached to employment than to political status and frequently do not constitute individual entitlements at all. Though Flora writes of the European welfare state, the same may be said for the welfare states of North America and Australasia.

Western European welfare states took their present form during the 'golden age of the welfare state', from the early 1960s to the mid 1970s (Flora, 1986, p.xii). Their foundations had been laid much earlier, in many cases in the period before World War I, and much of the present diversity of social policy institutions is a consequence of these varied histories. As differentiating factors in the formation of the welfare state, debate has identified the form and timing of industrial development, demographic change, cultural and religious tradition, political parties and class alliances, and bureaucratic interest within the state. Differences in timing and sequence of institutional development are of paramount importance. (In addition to Flora, 1986, see Esping-Andersen, 1985, 1990; Myles, 1989; Baldwin, 1990; Skocpol and Ikenberry, 1983).

More clearly than other welfare state functions, income support was a product of industrialisation and politics of class interest and alliance. Flora (1986, p.xx) points to three factors as significant in the shaping of income support arrangements: the homogeneity or heterogeneity of the blue collar workers in manufacturing, their ties to the farmers, and their relationship to the white collar employees. Esping-Andersen (1990) identifies universalism in social benefits with class alliances and the transcendance of the narrow,

22

short term 'ghetto strategy' in working class politics in favour of solidarity with other groups. Baldwin's (1990) interpretation refines the class thesis, showing that class interests have been mediated by the frameworks of risk pooling in social insurance arrangements. These risk groups correspond only partly to class groups. Thus the interests of middle class, white collar and self-employed groups have often had critical influence on the shape of income support arrangements.

The study has drawn on two international data sets developed for comparative international research. These are the Luxembourg Income Study (LIS) and the International Social Survey Programme (ISSP). These have made it possible to compare the incomes of the aged in countries whose income support systems give expression to universality and selectivity in various ways and the structure of political opinion which lies behind the welfare states of which they are part.

Six countries included in the LIS data set have been chosen as giving expression to universality and selectivity to various degrees and in the context of larger pension systems of different kinds. These are Australia, (West) Germany, the United States, the United Kingdom, Norway and Sweden. All have data available from the 'second wave' of LIS covering years in the mid-1980s, between 1984 and 1987 in the case of these six countries. Of these countries, all but Sweden were included in the 1990 'Role of Government' wave of the ISSP, upon which most of the attitudinal component of the study is based. Although the ISSP addressed the same subject matter in its 1985 wave, more contemporaneously with our income data, this earlier data set did not include either of the Scandinavian countries, and is therefore reduced to a subsidiary role in the analyses.

With almost all pensions subject to a test of means, Australia was an appropriate exemplar of selectivity. Norway and Sweden were chosen as exemplars of universality on the 'citizenship' model. These countries offer a basic level of income support on the ground of 'citizenship', effectively defined as residence. The United Kingdom was an interesting inclusion because it has close parallels with the Scandinavian countries in providing a universal, flat rate allowance while also making substantial use of means-tested benefits. Germany and the United States were included as examples of universality based on wage-related social insurance. In fact, the public pension schemes of these six countries typically combine elements of two or three of these principles. While universality is the dominant principle in five of the countries, there are also means tested elements in all of these. These are more significant in the UK than in the other four countries, but are also more significant in universalist Scandinavia than is often supposed.[1] Income support arrangements in the six countries chosen for the study are described in greater detail in the discussion to follow.

Patterns of welfare state development

In the development of income support, the most fundamental differentiation was that between the social insurance basis adopted in countries of continental Europe and the greater emphasis on need and citizenship in the systems developed in Britain and Scandinavia. Social insurance forms the core principle of the German welfare state. Rooted in the labour market, benefits are 'earned' through individual contributions, and their levels are earnings-related so as to maintain market inequalities in the system of public transfers (Alber, 1988, p.100). Bismarck sought to introduce German social protection to stabilise a newly forming industrial working class and to pre-empt its mobilisation as a mass political force. Its framing as insurance was, however, a departure from the patriarchal tradition of etatism. This was the result of a compromise with an emergent liberal bourgeoisie, which shaped social insurance to embody principles of individual responsibility and self-help. The same is true of its finance by employers and employees, with only a limited fiscal role for the state. Its fragmented corporatist character was built as new schemes were created to incorporate an increasing range of class groups. The key principles of German social provision were reconfirmed in postwar redevelopment under the rubric of the social market economy. Alber identifies these as fragmentation of programs, emphasis on cash benefits, and reliance on social insurance (Rimlinger, 1971; Alber, 1986; Myles, 1989).

Flora (1986, p.xx) identifies the citizenship principles of British and Scandinavian social protection with differences in the timing of industrialisation and the structures of class and party. In Britain industrial transformation was well advanced and parliamentary authority and mass democracy established before the turn of the century when a Liberal government embarked upon limited modernisation of social protection. Responding to labour militancy and social liberal reform movements, welfare measures were aimed at the respectable working class and included means-tested age pensions and limited social insurance for sickness and unemployment (Gilbert, 1966, pp.159-289; Thane, 1982, pp.61-3; Hill, 1990, pp.18-21). The shift towards a model based on citizenship came with World War II and the wave of social policy development generated by the Beveridge Report. Though legislated under Labour auspices, British establishment of a 'welfare state' reflected considerable interparty and bureaucratic consensus, driven in part by widespread popular support. Its

24

distinguishing features were comprehensiveness in needs and social groups covered, national pooling of social insurance risks and rewards, and flat rate benefits as a national minimum standard of wellbeing. Its liberal character was to be maintained through a grounding of provision in contributory insurance with a national minimum standard of wellbeing to be supplemented by voluntary private provision. The system was to be underpinned by means-tested public assistance (Thane, 1982, pp.223-69; Parry, 1987).

The citizenship basis of income support was interpreted more broadly in Scandinavia. Industrialisation came late in both Norway and Sweden, but in Sweden an organised working class had emerged by the end of the nineteenth century. Agriculture nevertheless continued to dominate Scandinavian economies until well into the twentieth century, in Norway as smallholder farming but in Sweden also including middle and large scale enterprises. Both countries also had rural working classes. Mass democracy was established earlier in Norway than in Sweden, where the government was not responsible to parliament until 1917, and universal suffrage not established until 1921. The distinctive basis of the Scandinavian welfare state is identified with a class compromise between the industrial workers and small farmers. Ironically the first precursor of Scandinavian social citizenship, the universal, tax funded age pension introduced in Sweden in 1913, owed less to the Social Democratic Party than to agrarian interests. A move to introduce similar provision in Norway failed. The distinctive Scandinavian model was forged in the wake of World War II on a basis established in the 1930s. In Sweden, a coalition government established universal, flat rate pensions for the aged and disabled and a general child allowance. In Norway an old age pension had been introduced in 1936 under the aegis of Labour government but with the support of all parties. The scheme was universal, but was based in part on contributions from income earners, and benefits were flat rate and means tested. After the war this and other early social insurance provisions were extended and modified, with universal coverage a central principle and means tests for the age pension abolished. It was with these postwar measures that the distinctive features of the Scandinavian model were put in place. In this first stage, these comprised a comprehensive system of universal social protection on the basis of flat rate benefits (Olson, 1986; Kuhnle, 1986; Alestalo and Kuhnle, 1987; Esping-Andersen and Korpi, 1987; Baldwin, 1990).

Both Australia and the United States have been considered exceptional cases in the formation of the welfare state, and to some extent both have remained so. Australia began to take much the same path as Britain and Sweden, establishing a flat rate, means-tested age pension early in the

25

century. Primary production dominated its economy, hence much of its working class was based in the countryside. Democratic institutions had been established early, and economic depression, industrial and political turbulence gave rise to the Australian Labor Party. The pension owed much, nevertheless, to New Liberal and protectionist support in the Parliament. Although the country has debated departures from this model, primarily social insurance, over a number of periods since, development has in fact continued to build on this basis. During and after World War II the system was expanded to include (then) universal child allowances and a system of categorical pensions and benefits. Funded from taxation, these entail eligibility for all, but entitlement is subject to a relatively generous test of means. Thus Australian exceptionalism lies in the rejection of universality in either its Scandinavian or its German social insurance form (Kewley, 1973; Shaver, 1991).

A variety of explanations have been offered for the late development of American income security. Skocpol (1992; see also Skocpol and Ikenberry, 1983) attributes the failure to establish an old age pension at the turn of the century to the early establishment of male suffrage and the spread of civil war pensions to Union veterans through patronage politics. Reformers were unwilling to support an expansion of state power likely to become a basis of further patronage. Quadagno (1988) stresses the uneven development of the American economy and regional conflict between the industrial north and the agricultural south, the weakness of national government, and divisions between industrial and craft unions. The Depression and populist pressures of the Townsend movement impelled the legislation of social security by the federal government during the 1930s, establishing a two-tier framework of social insurance for unemployment and retirement and means-tested social assistance for the aged poor and the children of indigent parents. The shape of American provision, most particularly in social insurance for the aged, faithfully reflected the influence of big business and welfare capitalism in the strength of liberal ideology of self-help. The retention of control by the states over provision other than social insurance for the aged followed from regional differences and the political power of the southern states (Quadagno, 1988; Rimlinger, 1971).

By the end of the second world war, then, the foundations of modern welfare states had been built even in those nations slowest to develop them. These foundations took a variety of forms. The conservative model evolving from the legacy of Bismarck is commonly contrasted with the liberal or reformist model[2] associated with citizenship (Flora, 1986, p.xx; Baldwin, 1990, pp.58-61), while Esping-Andersen's (1990) influential threefold typology of social policy regimes makes a further distinction between liberal and social democratic types. American social security has been variously identified as in the Bismarckian (Myles and Quadagno, 1997) and liberal (Esping-Andersen, 1990) moulds. Antipodean developments stood apart from all, clinging more closely to the social assistance origins of social security provision (Castles, 1985). During the postwar period welfare states grew within their diversity, but there was also some convergence among them. Flora (1986, pp.xx-xxv) describes this period as one of 'growth to limits'.

In West Germany, postwar reconstruction brought major extensions in social spending during the 1950s. This was followed by a period of consolidation with only moderate growth during the 1960s, and expansion again in the first half of the 1970s. While much of this growth represented the rounding out of health and education services in a system previously dominated by social insurance, new income maintenance programs were also introduced, including child, housing and education allowances. Proposals for fundamental reform of the conservative German welfare system were mooted in the 1950s but were blocked by political division. In the result, the expansion of the German welfare state largely confirmed its historical contours. This was particularly true in the case of age pensions, which have continued to be based on wage-related social insurance entitlements 'earned' through contributions. As the system expanded there were, however, significant changes within this framework, some of which modified it to make German social provision for low income groups more closely resemble that of other countries. The purpose of age pensions was redefined from subsistence to income maintenance, with benefits significantly increased and indexed to wage changes; accordingly, benefits became the major source of income in old age. Entitlements under workers' and employees' schemes were equalised, and pensions more closely linked to contributions. Later, a minimum pension component was introduced, raising benefits for low income groups. Voluntary membership became available to previously non-insured groups, particularly the self-employed and housewives. At the end of the 1960s income limits for compulsory coverage in employees' funds were abolished (Alber, 1986, 1988).

The German welfare state entered a period of 'austerity' following the recession of the mid-1970s, with both social-liberal and bourgeois governments attempting to hold rates of growth in social spending in line with the rate of growth of GDP. Cutbacks were sharpest in social security and education (Alber, 1988, pp.104-9). Pensions were curtailed through repeated modification of pension formulae and the postponement of annual adjustment of levels. However the pension schemes supporting the aged proved less vulnerable to cuts than did other social programs, and

27

pensioners generally maintained parity with the net incomes of the organised workforce through the period. Alber attributes their relative security to the political importance of pensioners as a large electoral group in and the view of their contributory entitlements as earned or deserved. The value of social assistance benefits declined in the same period (1988, pp.111-14).

Postwar social expenditure and provision grew less dramatically in the United Kingdom than in Germany. The range of benefits changed little in the period to the mid-1970s, the main extensions being the replacement of family allowances and child tax concessions with child benefit and the means-tested family income supplement. There was also an incremental growth in the importance of the social assistance safety net, which came during this period to serve as a permanent fallback for coverage deficiencies in the framework of national insurance. However the period did see a significant departure from the Beveridge tradition of flat rate contributions and benefits. This was rehearsed initially in the introduction of limited national superannuation in the mid-1960s and more substantially in the mid-1970s with the introduction of a supplementary tier of income-related pensions paralleling the development of occupational superannuation among white collar employees. The State Earnings Related Pension Scheme (SERPS) allowed individuals in private schemes providing equivalent protection to opt out (Perry, 1986; Baldwin, 1990, pp.232-47; Hill, 1990, p.39).

The election of the neoliberal Thatcher Government in 1979 put the Beveridge design of social policy under much greater challenge. Pressures to constrain expenditure in the face of increasing unemployment and an ageing population were compounded by a sharp ideological shift to economic liberalism. The new policy constellation favoured real reductions in expenditure, cuts in benefit levels, an increase in selectivity, concentration on improving work incentives and an extension of privatisation. The Fowler Review, commissioned in 1985, reasserted the importance of the means-tested elements in the social security system as a whole. The Thatcher program was achieved only in part, and up to the mid-1980s had much more significant effects on provision for unemployment and sickness than for the aged. Bradshaw concludes that the bulk of non-means-tested provision for the aged remained intact, though benefit levels were affected by the replacement of uprating by movements in wages with uprating by price levels (Bradshaw, 1993, pp.43-5). The most significant effects on provision of retirement income came through changes in SERPS. After an attempt to abolish the scheme failed, it was weakened and policy incentives instituted to encourage opting out in favour of private insurance. While Bradshaw views the structure as unchanged in important respects, Hill regards the historical endurance of the Beveridge framework as in question in the longer term. Walker suggests that the politics of old age have been fundamentally changed (Bradshaw, 1993, pp.43-5; Hill, 1990, pp.53-64; Walker, 1991, pp.27-9).

The welfare states of Norway and Sweden reached their full development in this period. Provisions in education and health were expanded in both countries. Pension levels were also increased, and retirement ages reduced. Olson (1986, p.18) notes that increases in the value of age pensions enabled Swedish pensioners to live on their pensions for the first time, albeit at a low standard. In both countries these pensions were complemented by means-tested housing allowances. The most significant development in both countries, however, was the development of a second tier of income support to the aged during the 1960s, supplementing universal, flat rate pensions with compulsory, earnings-related provision. In Sweden there was also a further phase of expansion associated with the development of manpower policy. This had ramifications for the aged in further reductions of pensionable age and the extension of entitlements to housing allowances to all age groups. It was also associated with extended benefits to families including parental leave provisions and tax credits to home owners. In Norway it was associated with extensions to unemployment and occupational injuries compensation. Benefits to families included the extension of universal child allowance to cover the first child (Olson, 1986; Kuhnle, 1986; Nielsen, 1991).

The economic problems of the 1970s had comparatively little effect on Norway and Sweden, and the welfare states of both survived the 1980s largely intact (Stephens, 1995, p.1). The Swedish welfare state had come under attack at the end of the 1970s, but the bourgeois parties that replaced the long ruling social democratic governments to the early 1980s did little more than halt the rise in social expenditure. Back in office, social democratic governments maintained that the 'mature' Swedish welfare state did not need to grow further (Olsson, 1988, pp.60, 87; Stephens, 1995, p.15). The major cash benefit programs went largely unchallenged, the main cutback to aged provision being reduced support for early retirement. Expenditure on wage-related pensions continued to grow, driven by the maturation of the system and the growing number of persons, including many women, having pension rights. There was also strong growth in private pensions among a wealthy minority (Olsson, 1988, pp.72-4). With the economy cushioned by oil revenues, Norwegian welfare politics were even more tranquil. Provisions were affected only by the longer running deterioration in the basic pension in favour of income-related payments (Nielsen, 1991).

The American social security program grew slowly over the first two postwar decades. Incremental changes extended coverage, improved benefit levels and reduced the retirement age for women. Universal health insurance for the aged was added in the early 1960s. The main development of American welfare capitalism during this period was, however, the growth and spread of occupational welfare in private pensions. The late 1960s and early 1970s saw a dramatic round of further development fostered by an alliance of the social security administration with organised labour. Social security provision was reshaped from a poverty program to a retirement wage, bringing it closer to European provision. These developments included increased contributions and benefit levels, a higher wage base, and tying benefit levels and wage parities to movements in prices and earnings. In the same period the means-tested tier was transferred from state to national level, establishing a secure national floor to income security for the aged (Achenbaum, 1986, pp.54-60; Quadagno, 1988, pp.149-53, 171). Quadagno (1991) argues that this was a turning point in the history of the American welfare state, incorporating the middle class in a solidaristic policy agenda.

Coming into office at much the same time as the Thatcher government in the United Kingdom, the similarly neoliberal Reagan administration attempted to halt the late growth of the American welfare state. The expansions of the early 1970s and the effects of high inflation on indexed benefit levels had resulted in greatly increasing expenditure. Meanwhile rising unemployment and declining real wages were constricting revenues, raising the prospect of a shortfall in the 1980s. Attempts to cut back income support to the aged had begun in the late 1970s. After an initial round of cuts was successfully resisted in 1981, a second series was implemented in 1983 under the threat of the program failing. Balancing the demands of liberals and conservatives, these included delayed indexation, the extension of coverage to federal workers, increased tax rates, the taxation of benefits for upper income retirees, and measures to curb early retirement. The early 1980s also saw cutbacks to universal health care for the elderly and the extension of tax support for private retirement savings. Much deeper cuts were applied to health and welfare programs directed to sole parents, the working poor and other low income groups (Achenbaum, 1986, pp.61-102; Quadagno, 1991; Gilbert, 1988, p.296).

Australia's rejection of social insurance in favour of categorical means-tested, flat rate pensions and benefits was confirmed in the postwar period. However, the long period of conservative government from 1949 to 1972 saw the progressive weakening of Australian residualism. Extensions of provision in health, education, housing, aged care and universal child allowances made middle income groups significant beneficiaries of social expenditure. Means testing for income support, most significant in the case of the age pension, was liberalised repeatedly. By the early 1970s the means test was remarkably generous, with almost two-thirds of the age-eligible population qualifying for part pension, though its value had been declining since the mid-1960s. The pension was universal for persons aged over 70 for a brief period during the 1970s, with pensions made taxable. The turning point came in the brief period of Labor government in the early 1970s, when rapid rises in public expenditure coincided with sharp rises in both inflation and unemployment. Cutbacks in eligibility and real benefit levels increased in pace and severity under the conservative government that followed its dismissal, and were greatest in assistance to the unemployed. The means testing of income support to the aged began incrementally, with an income test applied to indexation increases. The incoming Labor Government reasserted it as policy in 1983, in association with reforms to the tax treatment of private pension income and a commitment to higher parity of pension levels with wages (Kewley, 1973; Shaver, 1991).

As reflected in their provisions for income support in old age, the welfare states of these six countries have developed a variety of models. All have an underpinning of means-tested entitlements to protection against poverty in old age, the historical legacy of poor law and social assistance provision. Australia built an extended but still selective income support system on these foundations. In the OECD schema (1988a, p.17) Australia is classified with New Zealand and Iceland as having a 'basic' type of pension system. Germany and the United States have replaced means-tested entitlements with systems of earnings-related social insurance for all but small minorities of aged persons, and are grouped with most other European countries and Japan in the OECD classification of 'insurance' types of pension system. The legacy of Bismarck is strongest in (West) Germany, where there has been little development of private pension provision. The legacy was given a liberal inflection in the welfare capitalism of the United States, where the system has preserved substantial scope for private pensions to be delivered as occupational welfare. The United Kingdom, Norway and Sweden have universalised the entitlement to social protection, later supplementing it with wage-related social insurance. The OECD classifies Canada, Denmark, Finland, and Ireland as having similarly 'mixed' types of pension system. Within this category, arrangements in the UK differ significantly from those in the two Scandinavian countries. The universalism of the UK is defined in the market-based terms of social insurance, while that of Norway and Sweden is associated with residence and citizenship. The supplementary tier

31

of income-related provision is far more substantial in Norway and Sweden than in the UK.

Income support to the aged in the mid-1980s

This section describes provisions for income support to the aged in these six countries.[3] These descriptions apply to the income support systems of the six countries as they operated in the mid-1980s. Changes in income support provisions implemented since the mid-1980s in these countries are described briefly in a postscript at the end of the chapter.

(West) Germany

German social provision is framed in the terms of the 'social market economy', in which the 'social state' has a positive responsibility to ensure a decent standard of living and social justice, including income security. Its role is to supplement the market, and to compensate for market failures in the distribution of resources without, however, weakening the incentive structure of the free market economy. In this conception, the state is not responsible for promoting material equality among its citizens. Benefits are designed to preserve relativities of status and income between social groups over the life cycle (Zapf, 1986, p.132; Alber, 1986, p.4).

As noted above, income support in old age is provided through compulsory social insurance. While coverage of employed persons and their dependants is comprehensive,[4] provision itself is fragmented among a series of parallel occupational funds. Wage earners and salaried employees are covered in separate funds, though these are regulated and their provisions are identical. Civil servants also have separate provision. Uncovered persons such as non-working housewives and aliens with long term residence can join a fund on a voluntary basis under certain conditions.

Provisions are funded through contributions by employees and employers, with a further subsidy from government. Employers contribute approximately 9.35 per cent of their payroll expenses, while insured persons contribute about 9.35 per cent of gross earnings up to a ceiling, with self-employed persons contributing twice this amount. Males are eligible to claim benefits at age 63 after 35 years' contributions, or at age 65 after 5 years. Women are eligible at age 60 with 10 years' contributions in the previous 20 years.

Old age pensions are intended to maintain the standard of living attained in working life in old age, and are strongly earnings-related. The amount of pension payable is a function of the contribution record and the level of earnings of the insured person. According to Alber (1987, p.253), the formula results in an old age pension equal to 60 per cent of average earnings for a worker with a contribution record covering 40 years and an earnings record corresponding to the average income of all insured persons: in 1983 a worker in this situation would have received DM 15,267 per year. There is no minimum benefit. Survivor's pensions are paid to the widows and orphans of the insured. Broadly, these provide amounts equivalent to the old age pension for three months, and 60 per cent of that amount thereafter. Pensions are indexed annually to reflect increases in average earnings from employment (Alber, 1987, 253-4). In 1984, 95 per cent of aged married couples and 97 per cent of aged single females received income from social insurance.

Many employers also offer supplementary private pension plans providing additional benefits in retirement or disablement or to survivors. Some two-thirds of the workforce are covered by private schemes (Alber, 1987, p.251).

German social insurance is underpinned by means-tested social assistance funded by local and state government and administered by local authorities. Cash benefits are granted on a regular basis, or as a lump sum to meet a specific need.[5] Alber reports that in 1983 a married couple over 65 were entitled to regular social assistance benefits if their income fell below DM 745 per month after the cost of housing was paid; the assistance system then supplements family income to bring it to this level (Alber, 1987, pp.281-3). In 1984, three per cent of aged couples and 12 per cent of single females received income from means-tested benefits.

United Kingdom

The UK has evolved three tiers of income support to the aged. These are contributory national insurance, providing flat rate social insurance benefits, a thin layer of supplementary earnings-related insurance, and a safety net of means-tested benefits. As noted above, these arrangements reflect the Beveridge legacy in a liberal model of citizenship. Income support in old age is understood as an entitlement to a basic income, available as of right, but designed so as to ensure scope for the reward of effort in employment and saving.

National insurance is compulsory for all employees, including the self-employed, who are resident in the UK. Married women in employment, for many years permitted to opt out and be covered by their husbands' insurance, have been required to participate in their own right since 1977. Some others may contribute on a voluntary basis. Coverage is optional for employed persons earning less than the minimum weekly income level and for some self-employed persons. Contributions of employers and employees are earnings-related, subject to a maximum contribution level, with funding further supplemented by government. Additional earnings-related coverage is provided through the State Earnings Related Pension Scheme (SERPS), with employers having the option of 'contracting out' their employees for equal or better protection through a regulated private fund. Benefits are financed from contributions at graduated rates from employees and employers, supplemented by government. In 1986, employer contributions to national insurance and SERPS together, i.e. where no contracting out had taken place, ranged from five to 10.45 per cent of the employee's gross earnings up to a ceiling of £285 per week, and employee contributions from five to nine per cent to the same ceiling.

The retirement pension covers men aged 65 and women aged 60 years or more. National insurance benefits are flat rate, and entitlement depends on the number of years for which minimum contributions were paid and the length of working life. The number of years needed for a full pension is reduced in respect of periods spent in the care of a child or an elderly or disabled relative. On 1 July 1986, benefits were paid at the rates of £38.70 per week for a single person and £61.95 for married couple. Partial pensions may be paid, but no pension is payable if entitlement is less than one quarter of the full pension. A non-contributory pension funded from general revenue is available at the age of 80 years to those ineligible for a national insurance pension or receiving pension at a low rate. In 1986 the maximum value of this was £23.25. SERPS benefits are based on contributions over a twenty year period, after which they are to represent 25 per cent of the covered annual earnings (between upper and lower limits). Because the scheme began only in 1978, full entitlements will not be payable until 1998, and entitlements in 1986 were small.[6] Pensions are adjusted to changes in prices but not in wages, and are taxable as ordinary income. In 1986, 99 per cent of aged couples and 100 per cent of aged single women received social insurance benefits.

Social insurance is underpinned by a third tier of social assistance, through which income support and housing benefits are provided to the aged. These benefits are subject to means tests on income and assets, and are payable in addition to national assistance. Receipt of these payments is widespread. In 1986, 43 per cent of aged couples and 74 per cent of aged single women in the UK received means-tested benefits.

Most companies operate private pension arrangements providing retirement pensions and associated benefits for some or all of their employees. These are subject to government regulation and supervision. In 1983, 52 per cent of retirees received an earnings-related occupational pension, concentrated in white collar occupations (Parry, 1987, p.171).

The income support arrangements of Norway[7] and Sweden exemplify the Scandinavian model of the welfare state, the hallmarks of which are universalism and egalitarianism (Erikson, Hansen, Ringen and Uusitalo, 1987, pp.vii-viii). Like those in the UK, Norwegian income support provisions for the aged have three tiers of provision. In Norway these comprise a minimum, flat rate pension provided to all citizens and additional earnings-related social insurance, underpinned with means-tested social assistance.

The basic pension is a universal flat rate entitlement available to all residents from the age of 67.[8] Entitlement to a full pension requires residence of 40 years after the age of 16, but a reduced pension is payable after a minimum period of residence of three years. All claimants are also entitled to a compensation benefit introduced in 1970 to adjust for the effects of value-added taxation. Employees and self-employed workers earning over a basic amount are also covered by a supplementary insurance scheme providing earnings-related benefits. The scheme is compulsory for all those earning over a basic amount for a minimum period of three years. Those not receiving the earnings-related supplement or receiving only a small such payment are eligible for a special supplement.

The National Insurance Scheme (NIS), of which age pensions are part, is funded from contributions by employees, employers and government. In 1984 employee contributions were 4.4 per cent of assessed taxable income plus 5.9 per cent of gross earnings, with higher contributions applying to the self-employed. Employer contributions vary according to geographical region from 6.0 to 16.8 per cent of gross earnings of every employee.

The level of the basic pension is set annually by parliament and is not indexed automatically. The supplementary wage-related benefit is based on the number of contribution years, earnings in the best 20 years and a factor reflecting the aim that a full supplementary pension should amount to 45 per cent of average earnings above the basic pension level. Those too old to have built up contributions to the earnings-related scheme receive a special supplement. In May 1983 a pensioner qualifying for a full basic pension and not entitled to an earnings related supplementary pension was entitled to 34,739 NKR per year, or 38.5 per cent of average annual gross earnings for male industrial workers in 1980. If a pensioner has a spouse also entitled to a pension each received 28,060 NKR per year. (Kuhnle, 1987, p.72). In 1986, 94 per cent of aged married couples and 98 per cent of aged single women received social insurance payments.

Some supplements to social insurance benefits are means tested. The most important of these are housing benefits, and the spousal supplement payable if only one of the spouses receives a pension (Nordic Social-Statistical Committee, 1990, p.44). National Insurance provision is also underpinned by means-tested social assistance through municipal government. Levels of support vary, but are below minimum benefit levels of NIS. In 1986, 18 per cent of aged couples and 26 per cent of single females received income from one or more means-tested payments.

Occupational pension schemes are moderately well developed in Norway. In 1988, 59 per cent of white collar employees and 24 per cent of blue collar employees in private employment were reported to be covered by company-based pension plans (Hippe and Pedersen, 1988, cited in Øverbye, 1992, p.20).

Sweden

Like Norway and the UK, Sweden arranges income support to the aged in three tiers combining universal, income-related and means-tested elements. The basic pension provides universal, flat rate coverage to all persons aged over 16 years. A minimum pension requires residence in Sweden for three years or more. The pension is normally payable from the age of 65, but reduced benefits may be drawn from the age of 60. Similarly, retirement may be deferred until the age of 70 with the pension increased correspondingly. A special supplement is provided where a pensioner has no or low entitlement to a supplementary wage-related pension. The basic pension scheme is financed by contributions from employers, central government and municipal government (Olsson, 1987).

In addition, all employees have mandatory coverage in the earnings-related insurance scheme for National Supplementary Pension (ATP). Self-employed persons have the right to contract out of supplementary insurance, but only with respect to income derived from self-employment. Supplementary pensions are payable to persons who have earned more than a defined amount for at least three years. As with basic pension, eligibility for benefits begins at age 65 for men and women, with provision for early or late retirement with adjustment of the pension payable. Except for contributions from the self-employed, the scheme is wholly funded from contributions by employers (Olsson, 1987, pp.8-9).[9] In 1987 100 per cent of aged couples and aged single women received social insurance benefits.

In January 1982 the basic pension for a single person was 16,190 SKR per year, equivalent to 32 per cent of average disposable income for a single industrial worker. For a married couple where both were pensioners, the basic pension for each was 27,590 SKR, or 45 per cent of the disposable income of a married working couple with two children. Where the pensioner did not receive a wage-related pension, these amounts were raised to 25,276 SKR and 44,322 SKR for a single person and married couple respectively. These amounts were equivalent to 48 per cent of the average disposable income for a single industrial worker and 73 per cent of the average disposable income of a working couple respectively (Olsson, 1987, p.7). The amount of supplementary, earnings-related pension payable depends on income earned in previous years and the number of years of employment. Income is taken into account over a fifteen year period and only up to a ceiling figure. A full supplementary pension amounts to 60 per cent of the average pensionable income and requires an earnings history of 30 years (Olsson, 1987, pp.8-9).

In addition, retirement provision in Sweden includes occupational superannuation established by collective agreement. All public employees are entitled to coverage in one of these funds, as are most salaried employees and wage-earners in private sector employment. However, the system does not normally cover persons born before 1911 (Olsson, 1987, p.6).

Universal and earnings-related provisions are supplemented by several means-tested elements. Pensioners eligible for only the basic pension are also eligible for means-tested benefits in the form of a supplement for a dependent wife and for a municipal housing allowance. Social assistance provides for people not otherwise covered or where benefits are insufficient. In 1987, 13 per cent of aged couples and 49 per cent of aged single females received income from means-tested benefits.

United States

American income support in old age is provided through universal compulsory social insurance. American 'social security' covers those in the labour market, their spouses and survivors. Amendments in 1983 reduced a series of historical exclusions, among them federal civil servants and workers in non-profit organisations, but casual agricultural and domestic workers remain uncovered. Eligibility depends on past employment and contributions, with benefits payable from age 65 (62 subject to an earnings test) for both men and women.

The program is funded largely from matching contributions by employers and employees. In 1986 these were 5.7 per cent of payroll and earnings respectively up to a wage and salary ceiling. To qualify for benefits an individual must have met minimum contribution requirements approximately equivalent to ten years' of contributions. Beneficiaries below the age of 70 are subject to an earnings test. In 1986, 95 per cent of aged couples and 97 per cent of single females received income from social insurance.

Benefits are earnings-related, but the benefit formula is weighted so that low income groups receive a higher proportion of their pre-retirement income than do middle and high income groups. In addition benefits are subject to a maximum limit. An additional amount of 50 per cent of the pension payable to a fully insured pensioner is payable with respect to a dependent spouse aged 65 or more. In 1986 the average monthly benefit for retired workers was $US 488. Replacement rates at that time were estimated to vary from 27 to 57 per cent of pre-retirement income (LIS Institutional Database, US 86/79). Benefit levels are indexed annually in relation to prices.

Social insurance is underpinned by means-tested social assistance pensions paid by the federal government. These are means tested on income and assets. Further social assistance is available in the form of food stamps, subject to tests of income and assets. Five per cent of aged couples and 18 per cent of aged single women received means-tested payments in 1986.

Private pensions are widespread in the US for both salaried and hourly workers, and for unionised workers often form part of wage and salary bargaining. These plans are subject to regulation.

Australia

Income support to the aged in Australia is designed to ensure a minimum standard of income for aged individuals and couples without private resources. The age pension is payable at the age of 65 for males and 60 for females. There is also a service pension payable to those with eligible war service, on much the same basis as the standard age pension but available five years earlier. In addition, there are pensions paid in respect of injury related to war service. Some of these are more generous than the basic age or service pension, providing support to those with disabilities or their widows where the disability or death is accepted as associated with war service. These latter pensions are paid free of any means test.

Australian pensions are funded from general revenue, and there are no contributory requirements. In principle all persons of the requisite age and who have resided in Australia for at least ten years[10] are eligible to receive a pension. Actual entitlement, however, is subject to tests of both income and assets. The means test is applied to the combined income and assets of husbands and wives (de jure or de facto), but does not take into account the resources of children or other relatives. Entitlements are made individually, however, so that each partner in a couple receives half the assessed rate of pension in their own right. Benefits are flat rate for those fully entitled, but may be reduced by the effect of means tests. Single pensioners receive 60 per cent of the combined married rate. In 1985 the standard (single) rate of the age pension was $A97.90 per week, and the married rate $A81.65 each.

Separate tests apply to assets and income. The assets test excludes owner occupied housing and assets up to a ceiling figure, which is lower in the case of home owners than non-owners, and provides for the rate of pension paid to be reduced where assets are above this figure. The income test provides for some income, in 1985, $A30 per week for single pensioners and $A25 for each member of a couple, to be disregarded. Above that figure a 50 per cent taper rate applies, so that pension is reduced by one dollar for each two dollars of income. In 1985 pensioners receiving an amount at or near the full rate of pension were also entitled to a range of other benefits including free medical care and pharmaceuticals.[11]

In comparison with the means-tested provisions of other countries these tests are unusually generous in the level of means permitted to eligible claimants. The income cut out point for the married rate of pension was 89 per cent of adult average weekly earnings in 1985, while the assets test excludes only those with substantial private wealth. In the result, most persons in the eligible age groups receive some pension payment. In 1985-86, 75 per cent of aged couples and 91 per cent of single females received a full or part pension.

In the early 1980s fewer than half of Australians employed for more than 20 hours per week had private pension coverage. Coverage was rapidly extended through the 1980s when the trade union movement negotiated for the reform and expansion of occupational superannuation in lieu of wage increases (Walsh, 1991; McCallum, 1991). Between 1988 and 1991 coverage of full-time workers increased from 58 to 79 per cent, and of part-time workers from 19 to 44 per cent (ABS, 1991, p.6). However, this scheme is still in its early stages, and much of this coverage remains very thin, reflecting employer contributions of three per cent of salary.

Australia allows retiring members of superannuation funds to take all or part of their benefits in the form of a lump sum, and taxes these sums at concessional rates. This practice is widespread, so that occupational pensions may often appear as investment income in the incomes of the aged. At the end of the 1980s policy changes were implemented to make lump sums somewhat less attractive.

Postscript: developments since the mid-1980s

Germany The social security systems of the former West and East Germany were merged in 1993, following the reunification of Germany. Some provisions of the flat rate system of the former East Germany continue to apply in those jurisdictions. The Law on Pension Reform introduced further changes in response to population ageing and a declining birth rate. Taking effect in 1992, these altered the indexation formula to slow the rate of pension increase over time and began incremental restrictions on provisions giving access to pension benefits before the standard pensionable age of 65. At their completion in 2017, these restrictions will equalise the age provisions of men and women. A further rise in pension age was under consideration in 1996.

Pension credits for a three year period are provided to one parent for each child born after 1992. These credits are equivalent to employment at 75 per cent of the average earnings of covered workers. There is also a scheme paying contributions on behalf of people caring for others on a long term basis (Schmähl, 1993).

Cutbacks in social assistance were instituted in 1993, slowing increases in standard rates in the period to 1996 (Alber, 1996, cited in Stephens, Huber and Ray, forthcoming).

United Kingdom The decline in the value of the basic national insurance pension relative to wages has continued in the period following the mid-1980s. Basic pension alone is less than minimum levels of income set for receipt of social assistance, and the gaps between these have been widening. The basic pension alone is not intended to be high enough to cover housing costs, and expenditure on means-tested payments has risen sharply (Dilnot et al., 1994, pp.14-15, 202). Social assistance was restructured in 1988, when Supplementary Benefit was replaced by Income Support. This is a generic 'safety net' program of means-tested income supplements. Rates are composed of two elements, personal allowances and premiums for particular groups including age pensioners. In the case of age pensioners these premiums vary with age and disability. Additional means-tested housing assistance is available to recipients of Income Support for assistance with mortgage interest payments and tenants of private or public housing (Eardley et al., 1996, pp.391-404). In 1988 there were also changes to SERPS increasing the incentives for employers and employees to contract out of the scheme. There is provision for rebate of a proportion of the National Insurance contribution by both employers and employees. In 1993-94 this rebate was reduced from 7 to 4.8 per cent of earnings. The 1988 changes also extended the contracting out option to a further range of pensions, including both employer schemes and individual retirement accounts. These have had significant effects on the balance of public and private pension coverage (Dilnot et al., 1994, pp.16-28; see also Walker 1996, pp.16-17).

Sweden The slowed growth in aged income support of the 1980s was followed by radical changes in the 1990s. These have included cuts in pension levels and the abolition of early retirement provisions. The contributory ATP pension is being replaced with a social insurance pension funded from equal contributions by employers and employees of 9.25 per cent of payroll, with some pension recognition in respect of childhood and compulsory military service. The benefit formula will link benefits more closely to contributions over the whole of working life. In addition, the universal flat rate pension is being replaced by a guaranteed minimum pension provided only to those who are not eligible for a contributory pension. While contributory pensions are to be indexed to wages, the guaranteed minimum pension will be indexed to price changes. All pensions are to be taxable (Stephens, 1995).

United States Age of eligibility for social security pensions is to be gradually increased from 65 to 67 over the period from 2000-2007. Changes have also been introduced to make social security coverage mandatory for employees of state and local governments not covered under a retirement system.

Australia The age at which women become eligible for the age pension is to be increased from 60 to 65 over a twenty year period beginning in 1994. Changes have also been made in means test provisions to respond to claims that some types of investment were treated more favourably than others. The main developments in Australian retirement income policy have been aimed at encouraging the extension of private pension coverage and regulating its interaction with pension means test arrangements. This has included changes to pension income test provisions and to taxation treatment of income from private superannuation. Private pension coverage for most employees was mandated from 1992, with employers required to contribute a minimum of three or four per cent of payroll to regulated pension funds. Provision has been made for this contribution to rise to nine per cent by 2003, and for the introduction of employee contributions also towards the end of this period (Social Policy Division, 1993; Eardley et al., 1996, p.37).

Notes

1   The composition of income in the six countries will be discussed in greater detail below.
2   Often referred to as the Beveridge model.

41

3   Unless otherwise indicated, sources for the information presented in this section are Luxembourg Income Study Institutional Database and US Department of Health and Human Services (1990). Estimates of the proportion of the population receiving payment are calculated from the LIS data (see below).

4   Membership in an insurance fund is also compulsory for apprentices, unemployment beneficiaries and some groups of self-employed craftspersons and professionals.

5   The cost of nursing home residence is also supported through means-tested provisions. As residents of institutions are not included in LIS data, the coverage of means-tested benefits is understated in the analysis that follows.

6   In 1986 some retirees also had entitlements deriving from an earlier graduated pension scheme replaced by SERPS.

7   Unless otherwise indicated, the information reported in this section is drawn largely from Kuhnle (1987).

8   An option is provided to defer drawing the pension until the age of 70.

9   Employee contributions were introduced in the early 1990s. See below.

10   Persons who do not meet the residence requirements may qualify for a special benefit, subject to more restrictive conditions.

11   In 1993 these benefits were extended to all recipients of full or part pension.

3 Outcomes of universality and selectivity in the incomes of the aged

...the essence of the liberal European welfare state lies in the idea of basic rights of individuals to state-provided benefits as principal elements of their life chances. Security and equality are the welfare state's central objectives, i.e. the attempt to stabilize the life chances of, in principle, the entire population and to make their distribution more equal (Flora, 1986, p.xv).

The arguments about the relative merits of universal and selective provision of income support concern the appropriate means to achieve these linked ends in the institutional structures of the welfare state. This chapter reviews these arguments in the light of evidence about their outcomes in the incomes of aged couples and single females in the six countries.

Opportunities for quantitative comparative research on incomes have been greatly increased by the development of the Luxembourg Income Study (LIS) database. The LIS database comprises microdata from national surveys of income, expenditure or tax files which have been standardised to produce definitions of income and income components which, while far from perfect, are much more directly comparable than have been available in the past. The number of countries and 'waves' of data for similar years included in LIS has steadily grown since the commencement of the project in 1983 (Smeeding, O'Higgins and Rainwater, 1990; Mitchell, 1991).

The LIS project has made it possible to compare the roles of universality and selectivity in pension systems in the actual incomes of the aged populations of a growing number of countries. Because the principles of universality and selectivity are combined in the income support systems of most countries, it is their operation in combination that matters for the wellbeing of the aged. Moreover their effects depend on the interaction of income support provisions with income from other sources in the total income packages of the aged. Much past argument about the relative virtues of competing principles has compared policy choices in expenditure terms (Pampel and Williamson, 1989; see also Esping-Andersen, 1990), or on the basis of models working out the effects of various types of benefit on individuals or families of varying composition and income (see e.g. Bradshaw et al., 1993). The former are very inexact in the comparison of policy instruments. The latter usefully show the way policies are intended to work, but do not necessarily show how they work in practice. It is now possible, within the limitations of the LIS database, to compare income support systems and the provisions that comprise them on the basis of their outcomes. Such comparisons are best made on the basis of data on the outcomes of income support systems in the incomes of the aged.

The use of LIS data

Personal and income data for aged persons were taken from the LIS data set for each of these six countries. The population to be included from each country comprised aged individuals or couples. Among these, the populations included in the study were further limited to aged persons and couples in households of their own, where there were no other people present. This maximised the opportunity to compare like with like, but at the same time may have understated poverty by excluding individuals and couples whose low incomes force them to live with others. Inter-country comparisons need to be read with this limitation in mind. Individuals and couples whose gross incomes were zero or negative were also excluded.

In setting a lower age limit for inclusion in the study population it was necessary to compromise between the goals of having as large a population as possible and representing the population eligible for income support in each country. In the result, the age of 65 was chosen. By this age both men and women were eligible for income support in most countries, and the population to be included was defined as individuals and couples the head of which was aged 65 or more at the time of the survey. This definition was varied in the case of Norway where eligibility commences at age 67, and the population defined as individuals or couples with heads aged 67 or more.

Data were analysed on an income unit basis. The income unit, comprising a single adult or couple, was chosen as the unit of analysis because it broadly corresponds with the framework of income support systems in most countries.[1] This study presents comparative analysis of the incomes of two particular types of income unit, couples and single females. These have

44

been chosen as representing the types of income unit which are most common among aged people. They also capture important variations in the effects of different income support systems on income in old age, including the higher incidence of poverty among single aged women in many countries (Smeeding, Torrey and Rainwater, 1993, p.12). The number of couples and single females in the study population for each country are shown in the Appendix, with other technical information about the use of the LIS data set in the analysis for this research.

In order to keep the analysis as simple as possible, incomes have been compared only with those of other income units of the same type in the same country. Thus the benefit and other incomes of couples are compared with those of other couples, rather than with those of all aged income units in the same country. This has avoided the need to use equivalence scales, to which some of the comparisons undertaken are very sensitive. In consequence, however, the opportunity to compare the incomes of aged couples and single women with each other has been reduced. Nor has it been possible to avoid the use of equivalence scales altogether. These were required for analysis of poverty rates among the aged in the six countries, where the incomes of aged couples and single women had to be compared to those of the general population. The choice of equivalence scale and the sensitivity of the estimates to it are described below.

The model of income used in the study distinguishes private income, including private pensions, from income received as cash social benefits through the transfer system, and also distinguishes benefits from taxation. The model portrays the process of income formation as taking place in a succession of stages. The first two stages consist of *factor income*, including income from employment and self-employment and income from property, and *market income*, defined as factor income plus income from private pensions. *Gross income* is the sum of market income and income from transfers, within which social insurance and means-tested transfers have been distinguished.[2] Finally, *disposable (net) income* is defined as gross income less payroll and direct taxes, including social security contributions. The strength of this model is its capacity to elucidate the role of public transfers and taxes in modifying the distribution of income from private sources (Mitchell, 1991, p.15). It is, however, less than perfect in providing a 'counterfactual' against which to compare the redistributive effects of public transfers. This is because it assumes that the receipt of private income is independent of the nature and level of public support, when in practice these are interdependent. Because interactions between public and private income are likely to vary from country to country this weakness has to be borne in mind when considering inter-country comparisons.

National variations in the LIS data sets for Germany, Sweden and Australia have had some effect on the comparisons presented. In general, LIS data sets identify income from private occupational pensions, a component of market income, separately from income from social insurance transfers and one of the components added in the step from market to gross income. In the German and Swedish data sets, however, income from private pensions is not separately shown but included with income from social insurance transfers. The effect of this is to understate factor income and overstate the contribution of social insurance transfers in these countries as compared with others. These variations are more serious in the case of Germany, where private pension coverage is voluntary and largely limited to salaried workers, than of Sweden, where it forms part of collective wage agreements (Pestieau, 1992, pp.34-8). In the Australian data, income from the service pension awarded to armed services veterans with qualifying war service has been included in the measure of income from employment related pensions. Reflecting the ageing of the men and women who served in World War II, this income was substantial in 1985-86. This income is ambiguously public or private in nature. Its classification in the LIS schema reflects its direct association with employment, and it has been treated as a private pension in the present study. However, because the terms and conditions of the service pension parallel those of the public age pension, it is also often regarded as part of the framework of public income support. The implications of these variations for the interpretation of comparative evidence are noted in the text as relevant.

Wherever possible the definitions of variables used in data analysis have followed standard LIS conventions. The most important of these for the present study are set out in the Appendix. The main exception concerned Australian income from public pensions which, because it represents the main form of income support to the aged in that country, is coded in the same category as social insurance transfers elsewhere. For the purposes of the present study it was important for its selective character to be reflected and it was recoded as a means-tested transfer.

Universality and selectivity in practice

As has been noted, the frameworks of actual income support systems are much more complex than is often recognised in the debates about universality and selectivity in income support. While selectivity can be unambiguously identified with means-tested benefit allocation, universality is variously associated with eligibility for benefits on the basis of social insurance and social citizenship. The income support systems of most

46

countries combine at least two and often three of these elements. Moreover, these elements interact with income from other sources, so that the relative importance of universality and selectivity in income support arrangements also depends on (and in turn influences) the balance of income from public and private sources in the overall incomes of the aged in each country. This chapter begins with descriptive comparisons of the roles of universal and selective benefits and their place in the larger composition of income among the aged in the six countries.

Inclusiveness and coverage

The most direct expressions of universality and selectivity in income support lie in the spread of income from benefits of these kinds across the relevant population in each country. Claims made for universality have linked it with the shared status and experience of entitlement, while those made for selectivity have identified that principle with targeting and relative need. The coverage of benefits of each type, i.e. the proportion of the eligible population who receive income from a universal or selective benefit, gives an indication of the importance of each kind of benefit in the income support systems of the six countries.

Table 3.1 below shows the coverage of universal and selective forms of income support in the six countries. The first row of the table presents the proportions of aged couples and single females living alone who had received income of any amount from a social transfer payment in the survey period, including both universal and selective benefits. The table shows that the receipt of transfer income in old age approaches universality in all countries with the exception of Australia. Australian income support is provided on an overtly selective basis, and only three couples in four had income from a pension or benefit, compared to 95 per cent or more of couples in all other countries. It is notable that there was very little difference between the proportions of couples receiving income from public transfers in the social insurance countries, Germany and the US, and in those countries in which social insurance comes on top of a universal benefit, the UK, Norway and Sweden.

In all countries, the receipt of transfer income in old age was an even more universal experience among single females than couples. This group includes both women receiving retirement income in their own right and widows having entitlements as the survivors of their husbands. The greater universality of receipt says nothing about the level of such benefits, but only that the experience of claiming and receiving them is very widely shared.

Table 3.1

Coverage of income support: percentages of aged couples and single females receiving income from social transfers and means-tested transfers in six countries

	Australia (1985-6)		(West) Germany (1984)		United States (1986)		United Kingdom (1986)		Norway (1986)		Sweden (1987)	
	C	SF	C	SF	C	SF	C	SF	C	SF	C	SF
Receives social transfer income of any kind	75	91	97	99	95	97	99	100	98	99	100	100
Receives social insurance transfer income	0	0	97	99	95	94	99	100	98	99	100	100
Receives means-tested transfer income	75	91	3	12	5	18	43	74	18	27	13	49
Receives both social insurance and means-tested transfer income	0	0	3	12	5	15	43	74	18	26	13	49
Receives neither social nor means-tested transfer income	25	9	3	1	5	4	1	0	2	1	0	0

Income units with heads aged 65 or more (67 in Norway) and living in households with no other persons. Income figures are weighted and are based on weekly data for the United Kingdom and annual data for all other countries. Cases with negative or zero gross income have been excluded. C = couples, SF = single females.

Source: Luxembourg Income Study database.

The second row of the table shows the coverage of universal benefits in the six countries. These include both contributory social insurance payments and transfers made on the basis of residence or citizenship.[3] The coverage of universal benefits was virtually identical with that of social transfers as a whole, reflecting the reliance on benefits based on social insurance or citizenship as the basis of income support in all the countries except Australia. The only exception to this pattern is found among single females in the United States, where there were some women not receiving any income from social insurance transfers. In the other countries, coverage among single women was as high or higher than that among couples.

The coverage of means-tested benefits is shown in the third row of the table, and here there was much greater variation among the six countries. The spread of means-tested benefits was much wider in Australia than in the other countries, but receipt of these benefits was also widespread in the UK. Proportions of couples and single women receiving means-tested benefits were smallest in Germany and the United States, where the basis of universal income support is social insurance.

The receipt of selective transfers was generally more common in the three countries whose income support systems combine flat rate benefits with wage-related social insurance. In all six countries the coverage of means-tested benefits was markedly higher among single women than couples.

The fourth row of the table shows the percentages of couples and single women in each country who received both universal and selective transfers. These figures reflect the frequency with which means-tested benefits were used to supplement universal payments – as allowances for particular circumstances or to 'top up' low levels of entitlement, or as a safety net for those falling into gaps in the rules of eligibility for social insurance or citizenship payments. Australia aside, the proportions of those receiving means-tested payments closely matched the proportions receiving universal ones. This suggests that the predominant role of means-tested payments was to provide *supplementary* income, and that they were relatively little used as an *alternative* source of minimum income.

The last row of the table shows the proportions of aged couples and single females in each country receiving no income from transfers. Once again Australia stands out from the other countries, with one quarter of couples and almost one tenth of single women receiving neither universal nor selective forms of income support. The United States and Germany had somewhat larger proportions not receiving income support than the remaining three countries. The proportions of couples not receiving income support were generally greater than those of single women.

These measures of coverage show Australian and to a lesser extent also UK income support as clearly more selective than the systems of the other four countries. Among those four, they show means-tested benefits playing a smaller part in the social insurance universalism of German and US income support than in the mixed systems of Norway and Sweden, where universalism is defined by residence. The receipt of means-tested income support provisions was more common in the supposedly universal systems of Scandinavia than is often supposed.

The importance of universality and selectivity in income support depends not only on how widely these types of benefit are shared among the population but also on how significantly such benefits figure in the overall incomes of their recipients. That is, the picture of selectivity and universality in the benefit systems of these two incomes needs to be put in the context of income composition. As Table 3.2 shows, transfers made up different shares of the total incomes of the aged in the six countries considered here.

The table shows the composition of income among aged couples and aged single women calculated on an 'average share' basis. This entailed finding the fraction of each income component in gross income for each individual or couple and calculating the average of these fractions. While it provides a useful summary picture of the income profiles of the aged in each country, it is also subject to some qualifications. As an average measure, it does not show differences in the extent to which low and high income groups depend on income from earnings, investment and public and private pensions in each country. It is also necessarily artificial in certain respects, showing 'average' shares of income from sources that are not normally combined in the income of a single individual or couple. This is the case, for example, in countries where a retirement test precludes an individual receiving income from both social insurance benefits and a wage or salary.

As Table 3.2 shows, on average factor income made up as much as one quarter of gross income of couples in the United States and Australia and one fifth in Norway. Factor income made up smaller parts of the gross incomes of the aged in Germany and the UK than in Norway and Sweden, and comparatively larger parts of the incomes of the aged in Australia and the US. In all countries except Sweden it was more important in the incomes of couples than of single women. While cash property income was by far the most important component of factor income in most countries, wages and salaries were important in the incomes of aged couples in Norway and the United States.

Employment-related pensions were a further source of private income in Australia, the UK and the US. Private pensions were much more important in the incomes of couples than of single women in all these countries. As noted above, the high level of income from employment-related pensions in Australia reflects the inclusion of service pensions paid to war veterans. This is the main cause of the unusually large disparity between the incomes of couples and single females in this component of income. Private

50

Table 3.2

Composition of income: average share of each income component in gross income, couple and single female income units (percentages)

	Australia (1985-6)		(West) Germany (1984)		United States (1986)		United Kingdom (1986)		Norway (1986)		Sweden (1987)	
	C	SF	C	SF	C	SF	C	SF	C	SF	C	SF
Wages and salaries	4	1	3	1	12	4	3	1	10	3	7	1
Self-employment income	3	1	3	1	2	-1	1	0	2	1	0	1
Cash property income	20	15	6	4	19	18	10	7	8	5	7	11
Factor Income	26	16	13	5	33	20	14	8	20	9	15	12
Employment related pensions	22	5	*	*	15	9	19	10	7	6	*	*
Market Income	48	22	13	5	47	29	33	18	27	15	15	12
Social insurance transfers	0	0	86	91	51	65	62	63	71	82	85	80
Means-tested transfers	50	77	1	3	1	5	5	18	1	2	1	8
Private transfers	0	0	0	1	0	0	0	0	0	0	0	0
Other income	2	1	0	0	0	0	0	0	1	0	0	0
Gross Income	100	100	100	100	100	100	100	100	100	100	100	100
Payroll taxes	0	0	1	0	1	0	0	0	3	1	na	na
Direct taxes	4	2	1	1	5	3	7	3	12	5	29	21
Disposable (Net) Income	96	98	98	99	94	97	93	97	86	94	71	79

Income units with heads aged 65 (67 in Norway) or more and living in households without other persons. Cases with negative or zero gross income have been excluded. Composition of income calculated using average share method. C = couples, SF = single females.

Note: * Income from employment related pensions is included in income from social insurance transfers in data for Germany and Sweden.

Source: Luxembourg Income Study database.

pensions added little to the private incomes of both aged couples and single women in Norway. As noted above, the LIS data set for the mid-1980s does not distinguish income from public and private pensions in Germany and Sweden, and the inclusion of private pension income with public transfers has the effect of overstating somewhat the importance of public pensions in gross incomes in those countries. Kohl (1992, p.130) estimates that on average occupational pensions made up eight per cent of the household incomes of the elderly in Germany around 1980 and around 10 per cent in Sweden.

Social insurance (universal) transfers made up more than half of the gross incomes of the aged in all countries. These formed the largest share of income in Germany, Sweden and Norway, making up, on average, 86, 85 and 71 per cent of the gross incomes of couples respectively. At 65 per cent, social insurance transfers also formed the majority of income of aged couples in the UK, but were on average barely more than half the total incomes of couples in the United States. Because of their greater ages and lower factor incomes, social insurance transfers were more important in the incomes of aged single women than of couples in all countries except Sweden.

Calculated as a mean share in gross income, means-tested transfers were significant only in Australia and, to a lesser extent, the UK. Lacking the social insurance used in most other countries, the Australian income support system relied entirely on these benefits, means-tested transfers making up on average half the total income of aged couples and 77 per cent of the income of single aged women. In the United Kingdom these transfers represented on average 5 per cent of the incomes of couples and 18 per cent of those of single women. In the other countries, means-tested benefits played a negligible role in the incomes of aged couples or single women. As Table 3.1 showed, means-tested benefits went to quite large proportions of the aged in both Norway and Sweden. The marginal place of these benefits in the average composition of income suggests that these benefits typically had low values. The distribution of income from means-tested benefits will be discussed further below.

In summary, transfer payments, whether provided on a universal or selective basis, made up much larger shares of the incomes of the aged in Germany, the United Kingdom and Sweden than they do in Australia and the United States. These consist almost entirely of universal benefits in Germany, Norway and Sweden. Selective benefits play a very large part in the incomes of the aged in Australia, and are also more important in the incomes of the UK aged than in other countries.

Table 3.3 presents a typology of universality and selectivity in income support to the aged based on the type of income support system and the relative importance of means-tested transfers in the gross incomes of the aged. The classification of income support into basic, social insurance and mixed types follows the usage of the OECD (1988a, p.17), and reflects differences in the institutional character of income support arrangements. The patterns of coverage of universal and selective transfers discussed above broadly correspond to these types. The typology relates these to the average share of income from means-tested benefits in the gross incomes of aged couples and single females.

This typology identifies income support systems as more or less selective in terms of the importance of means-tested benefits in gross income. This gives an indication of the extent to which the aged depended on these benefits as compared with income from other sources, including universal benefits. It suggests that Australia stood apart from the other five countries in the selectivity of its income support arrangements. While the other five countries clustered together, they differed from each other in both the nature of their institutional arrangements and the relative importance of means testing. Among these, income support was clearly more selective in the UK than the other four countries, and for comparative purposes its arrangements might also be typified as substantially selective. The other four countries provide examples of universal income support on each of the social insurance and Scandinavian models.

Selectivity and poverty

Are selective income support arrangements more effective than universal ones in ensuring low levels of poverty? This question addresses the central claim made on behalf of selective benefits, that they direct resources to those in greatest need. This section compares the incidence of poverty among aged couples and single females in the six countries.

Inter-country comparisons of poverty necessarily sacrifice some of the precision with which poverty measurement can be tailored to the way of life in a single country in favour of a general standard which can be applied to a number of countries. The LIS data set has been designed with this latter purpose in view. Here we define poverty in terms of relative income standards within countries, comparing the incomes of the poor with those of others in the same society. Inter-country comparisons thus involve

Table 3.3
Typology of universality and selectivity in income support

Share of gross income subject to means testing	Basic income support	Social insurance	Mixed income support system
<5		Germany	Norway
<10		US	Sweden
<20			UK
<50			
50+	Australia		

Source: Based on OECD, 1988a, p.17 and Luxembourg Income Study database.

assessments against the same relative standard. One consequence is that the actual levels of income used to define poverty vary from country to country.

In practice, low income is most commonly defined as a fraction of median equivalent disposable income. Förster (1993, 11) argues that because it reflects the standard of living that is most widely shared in the society, median income provides a better reference point than average income. The sensitivity of the measure of poverty to the particular fraction chosen is determined by comparing the results of a series of poverty lines.

LIS data may be used to measure the significance of poverty in various countries with the use of both the 'head count' and 'poverty gap' methods (Mitchell, 1991). The first of these measures poverty by the number of individuals or families whose incomes fall below a given poverty line, while the second measures the aggregate shortfall of their incomes below the income necessary for them to reach the poverty standard. This book reports measures based on the head count method, counting the number of aged income units below a series of relative poverty lines. These measures have the virtue of simplicity and are less sensitive than poverty gap measures to data outliers such as households with zero or negative incomes. They do not show differences among countries in the degree of poverty experienced by those counted as below a given poverty line. Because head count measures are often sensitive to the particular level at which the poverty line is drawn, estimates are presented for poverty lines drawn at a number of levels.

As indicated above, the analysis has been designed to compare income units with others of the same two types, aged couples or single females, in the six countries. Measurements of poverty among these units nevertheless require the use of equivalence scales to adjust for the differing needs of families of different size and composition in the wider population with whom they are to be compared. Because comparisons of low incomes are very sensitive to the measures of equivalence applied, and are especially so in the case of the aged (Buhmann et al., 1988, cited in Mitchell, 1991, p.23; Förster, 1993, p.19), results are presented using two different equivalence scales. These are the OECD scale, which weights the first adult in an income unit more heavily than other adults and adults more heavily than children, and a simpler scale taking account only of family size and giving successively less weight to each additional member of the unit.[4]

The standards conventionally used to define poverty in comparative studies using the LIS data are equivalent disposable (net) incomes of 40, 50 and 60 per cent of the median equivalent disposable income of all families in the same country, including the non-aged. While essentially arbitrary, these standards do bear some relationship to the income levels regarded as defining poverty in some of the countries under consideration. The first, at 40 per cent of median equivalent income, is close to the United States poverty line, while the third, at 60 per cent of median equivalent income, approximates the Swedish existence minimum (Förster, 1993, 11).

Table 3.4 below shows the incidence of poverty among aged couples and single women at these three levels in the six countries. Figure 3.1 presents the same information in diagrammatic form. The upper panel of the table and the two left quadrants of the figure present estimates based on the OECD equivalence scale, while the lower panel and two right quadrants of the figure contain those based on the family size scale. The difference in poverty levels associated with the choice of equivalence scale is immediately obvious. The family size scale gives generally higher estimates of the incidence of poverty, with the difference more marked among single women than couples and increasing as the poverty line is drawn at higher levels. As the diagram makes clear, the choice of scale has little effect on the pattern of comparison between countries in the case of couples but shapes the comparison somewhat differently in the case of single women. One reason for this is that these scales assume different relativities in the needs and living costs of single people and couples. A second is that these scales assume different relativities in the needs and living costs of single people and couples. A second is that changing the equivalence scale affects not only the measure of equivalent incomes of aged income units but also the measure of median equivalent income for all units and hence the low income line with which they are compared. The measure of poverty among single aged women in Norway and Australia is clearly very sensitive to the point at which the poverty line is drawn, suggesting that pension levels cluster there in these countries.

Table 3.4

Percentage of couple and single female income units below poverty lines of 40, 50 and 60 per cent of median equivalent disposable income, two equivalence adjustments

| Country | Year | Percentage of median equivalent income | | | | | |
| | | 40 % | | 50 % | | 60 % | |
		C	SF	C	SF	C	SF
		OECD equivalence scale					
Australia	1985-6	2.6	1.3	4.0	3.5	30.4	43.5
(West) Germany	1984	3.1	1.9	6.9	5.9	14.4	13.6
US	1986	6.6	13.2	11.2	27.4	17.9	43.5
UK	1986	0.9	0.4	2.0	0.9	11.1	7.0
Norway	1986	0.2	1.7	1.3	4.5	16.0	34.5
Sweden	1987	0.2	1.6	0.7	2.7	4.0	11.9
		Family size equivalence scale					
Australia	1985-6	2.9	3.5	5.2	53.1	37.5	72.0
(West) Germany	1984	3.1	5.9	8.0	14.5	14.4	31.3
US	1986	7.4	25.7	11.7	45.0	18.8	57.0
UK	1986	0.9	0.7	2.4	8.7	13.1	28.7
Norway	1986	0.2	4.5	2.4	38.3	17.7	65.5
Sweden	1987	0.2	1.8	0.4	6.1	2.5	28.3

Income units with heads aged 65 (67 in Norway) or more and living in households without other persons. Cases with negative or zero gross income have been excluded. C = couple; SF = single female.

Source: Luxembourg Income Study database.

These estimates correspond reasonably closely to others based on LIS data, with one important exception. The incidence of poverty among the UK aged is widely believed to be substantially higher than is suggested by the results presented here. Measures based on the 'first wave' data for 1979 were considerably greater. Hedstrom and Ringen (1990) reported poverty rates (at 50 per cent of median equivalent income) of 16.2 and 22.0 per cent among those aged 65 to 74 and 75 and older respectively. Mitchell (1991) measured the incidence of poverty among the UK aged (also at 50 per cent of median equivalent income) as 15.6 and 17.8 per cent among single people and couples respectively. However, estimates based on 'second wave' data

Couples

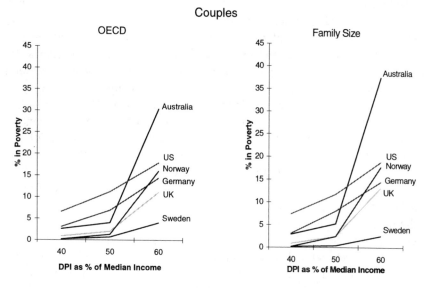

Single females

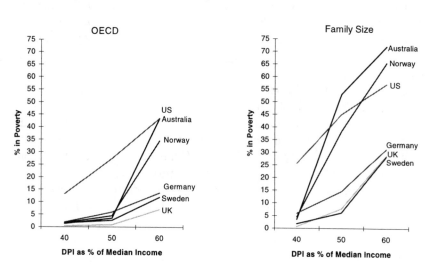

Figure 3.1   **Percentage of couple and single female income units below poverty lines of 40, 50 and 60 per cent of median equivalent disposable income, two equivalence adjustments**

Source: Table 4.

for 1986 are considerably closer to those reported here. Rainwater (1992, cited in Whiteford and Kennedy, 1995) estimated the poverty rate among older people (aged 60 and over) in the UK (at 50 per cent of median equivalent income) as 8.6 per cent, and Smeeding, Torrey and Rainwater (1993) found rates (at 40 per cent of median equivalent income) of 0.4 and 0.9 per cent among single elderly women and elderly couples respectively.

In a review of these findings, Whiteford and Kennedy (1995, pp.14-25) find a number of reasons for differences in measured poverty rates among the UK aged. They explain the apparent fall of poverty between 1979 and 1986 as the result both of actual improvement in the economic circumstances of this group and of differences in the way LIS data for the UK were constructed in the first and second waves. The incomes of older people in the UK had been rising over a long period, both in real terms and in the incomes of pensioners relative to those of non-pensioners. Hence it is likely that fewer were poor in 1986 than in 1979. However, this apparent fall in poverty is exaggerated by a number of methodological differences. Two of these concern the treatment of employee contributions to occupational pensions and tax relief for mortgage interest payments, both of which have the effect of increasing the apparent incomes of the aged relative to the rest of the population. Thirdly, Whiteford and Kennedy point out that these measurements are highly sensitive to variations in methodology, including the definition of the group of elderly to be included, the choice of unit of analysis, the equivalence scale that is used, and the point at which the poverty line is drawn. Measures for the UK (and also for Australia) are particularly sensitive to these variations.

The most important issue for present purposes is how these issues bear on the comparison of poverty among the aged in the six countries concerned. As Whiteford and Kennedy show, the 1986 LIS data set for the UK is more directly comparable with those for other countries than the 1979. One important difference remains, however, in the treatment of tax relief for mortage interest payments since 1983. In the UK, these are provided at source and their benefit reflected in lower mortgage repayments rather than in lower tax payments. The effect is to reduce the measured housing costs of house purchasers and to increase their measured income tax relative to their counterparts in other countries. It makes all those without mortgages look relatively better off, including most older people. Whiteford and Kennedy's own measure of poverty in the UK was similar to that shown in Table 3.4 at 40 per cent of median equivalent income, but was markedly higher at 50 and 60 per cent of median equivalent income.[5]

Whichever equivalence scale is used, the income support systems of all six countries brought all but a small minority of aged couples to the lowest poverty line of 40 per cent of median income. Using the OECD scale, less than one per cent of aged couples in the UK, Norway and Sweden had equivalent incomes below this line, and 2.6 and 3.1 per cent in Australia and Germany respectively. At 6.6 per cent, this level of poverty was more than twice as common among couples in the United States than Germany. With the exception of American social security, the income support systems of these six countries also brought the equivalent incomes of most aged single women above 40 per cent of median income. Again using the OECD equivalence scale, fewer than two per cent had equivalent incomes below this level in all five countries, while the American figure was six times higher.

The levels of poverty among the aged in the six countries grow more diverse as the poverty line is drawn at successively higher levels. At 50 per cent of median income (OECD scale), the percentage of aged couples in poverty was below two per cent in the UK, Norway and Sweden, but was 4.0 and 6.9 in Australia and Germany respectively. At 11.2 per cent, poverty among aged couples was markedly higher in the United States. Among single women, fewer than one per cent (OECD scale) of those in the UK had equivalent incomes of less than half of median income, compared to between 3.5 and 5.9 per cent in Sweden, Australia, Norway and Germany. At this level more than one single aged women in four in the United States was in poverty.

At the highest of the three standards, levels of poverty among aged couples were markedly higher in all countries and the variation among countries far greater. Again using the OECD scale, levels of poverty among aged couples ranged from a low of 4.0 per cent in Sweden to a high of 30.4 in Australia. At this standard, levels in Australia had overtaken those in the United States, where 17.9 per cent of aged couples had equivalent incomes of less than 60 per cent of median equivalent disposable income. In the UK, Germany and Norway poverty among aged couples ranged from 11 to 16 per cent.

When the poverty line is drawn at 50 and 60 per cent of median equivalent income, the incidence of poverty among aged single women was far higher than that among aged couples in most countries. The main exception was the UK, where the measurement based on the OECD equivalence scale shows 0.9 and seven per cent of single females to be in poverty at 50 and 60 per cent of median equivalent income respectively, compared to 2.0 and 11.1 per cent of couples.

While the choice of equivalence scale made little difference to the comparative picture of poverty among couples in these countries, it had a powerful effect on the estimation of poverty among aged single women. In the case of this group it has affected estimates not only of the level of poverty within countries but also the comparative relationships among countries. As noted above, the difference between these pictures is due to different assumptions about the relative living costs of single people and couples, and about the relative living costs of other family types in the calculation of equivalent incomes of the population at large. Because of this, the scales affect median equivalent income and hence the poverty line. In the case of Australia and Norway these differences have greatly increased the estimates of the number of single aged women whose equivalent incomes were below 50 per cent of median income.

As can be seen most easily in Figure 3.1, poverty among the aged is generally lowest in Sweden and the UK, and in Norway up to the 50 per cent of median income poverty line. Poverty is unambiguously highest in the United States except at levels above 50 per cent of median income, where it is high also in Australia and Norway. If the picture of single women given by the family size scale is set aside, there are two types of poverty profile over the range of poverty lines: in Sweden, the UK, Germany and the US the incidence of poverty rises slowly but steadily as the line is drawn at larger fractions of median income, while in Norway and Australia poverty is generally low below 50 per cent of median income but rises steeply at higher levels. This pattern stands out much more strongly when the profile of poverty among aged single women is drawn using the family size equivalence scale.

The answer to the question of whether selective income support arrangements do more than universal ones to minimise poverty is therefore 'not necessarily'. It is true that when the poverty line is drawn most austerely the levels of poverty in Australia and the UK were low, but so also were those of the universalist Scandinavian countries. The UK, with comparatively strong selective elements, had low levels of poverty at higher poverty standards, but so also did universalist Sweden. The social insurance universalism of Germany and especially the United States were, however, associated with comparatively high rates of poverty among the aged across the range of poverty standards.

Selectivity and the redistribution of income

Much contemporary support for selective benefits rests on the general belief that in concentrating expenditure on those with fewest other resources, arrangements of this kind do more than universal ones to redistribute income in favour of low income groups. This argument identifies them not only with the alleviation of poverty but with broader notions of social justice. However, not all evidence supports this proposition. Mitchell found that while Australian selective income support was the most efficient of the ten she studied in directing income support payments to the pre-transfer poor, the universal systems also transferred the bulk of their social security expenditures to the pre-transfer poor (1991, pp.81-92). Saunders' (1994, pp.110-19) results contradicted the general proposition. He found that Australia's highly targeted transfer system and the relatively selective one of the UK were less effective in reducing poverty among the aged than the universal and mixed benefit systems of seven other countries. He also showed the Australian and UK pension systems to be less generous than others having substantial elements of universality.[6]

The next subsection examines the way in which payments from universal and selective benefits affect the degree of inequality in the incomes of the aged in the six countries. It begins by describing the way benefit income from universal and selective transfers was distributed in relation to the gross incomes of aged couples and single women. It then turns to discussion of the role of universal and selective transfers in the redistribution of income among the aged. Finally, it puts the discussion of redistribution through universal and selective transfers in the context of how much national governments spend on income support.

The distribution of universal and selective benefits

Table 3.5 below shows how the total amount of income received in (universal) social insurance benefits was distributed among its recipients. The table shows the proportion of income from social insurance transfers which was received by the members of each quintile of gross income. For example, US aged couples in the bottom 20 per cent of the gross income distribution received only 15.1 per cent of all the social insurance benefits received by aged couples, while couples in the middle quintile received 23.4 per cent and couples in the top 20 per cent received 18.8 per cent.

As Table 3.2 showed, social insurance is by far the largest component in the incomes of aged couples and single women, making up on average between 51 per cent (US couples) and 91 per cent (Germany, single females) of gross income. The way in which income from social insurance benefits is distributed thus does much to shape the distribution of income among the aged.

Income from social insurance transfers was not evenly distributed among recipients, even in countries whose benefit systems have strong bases in universality. Income from social insurance transfers was quite unequally distributed in both Germany and Sweden, despite the existence of a universal minimum benefit provided as a right of citizenship in Sweden.

Table 3.5

Distribution of income from social insurance transfers among quintiles of gross income for aged couples and single females

Country	Year	Quintile of gross income					Total
		Lowest	Second	Third	Fourth	Fifth	

Couples

Country	Year	Lowest	Second	Third	Fourth	Fifth	Total
Australia	1985-6	na	na	na	na	na	na
(West) Germany	1984	10.8	17.4	20.8	23.8	27.1	100.0
US	1986	15.1	20.5	23.4	22.1	18.8	100.0
UK	1986	18.2	19.9	20.5	21.6	19.8	100.0
Norway	1986	14.8	18.5	20.7	21.5	24.5	100.0
Sweden	1987	12.0	17.0	19.5	21.9	29.6	100.0

Single females

Country	Year	Lowest	Second	Third	Fourth	Fifth	Total
Australia	1985-6	na	na	na	na	na	na
(West) Germany	1984	10.1	15.6	19.2	23.0	32.1	100.0
US	1986	11.5	19.2	21.5	24.5	23.3	100.0
UK	1986	19.0	19.2	19.6	19.9	22.3	100.0
Norway	1986	16.5	18.4	18.9	21.6	24.7	100.0
Sweden	1987	12.8	13.9	16.1	19.7	37.5	100.0

Income units with heads aged 65 (67 in Norway) or more and living in households without other persons. Cases with negative or zero gross income have been excluded.

Source: Luxembourg Income Study database.

However, transfer income was very equally distributed in the UK, where there is a flat rate minimum benefit and the wage-related tier above the minimum is very thin.

The table shows three different patterns in the distribution of social insurance benefits in these countries. In the UK, benefit income was very evenly distributed, with each group in total income getting approximately the same share of benefit income. In the US, social insurance benefits were distributed mildly in favour of middle income groups, at the expense mainly of the bottom quintile but also of the top quintile to some extent. In the other three countries income from social insurance benefits went disproportionately to higher income groups. This pattern was more marked in Germany and Sweden than in Norway.[7] In Germany, for example, the members of the lowest income group received only 10.8 per cent of total income from insurance transfers while those in the highest income group received 27.1 per cent (couples), almost three times as much. Differences among countries in the distribution of social insurance benefit income among aged single women were similar to but more pronounced than those among couples. In several countries the share of benefit income received by the top gross income quintile of women was markedly higher than that received by couples. This reflects the lower non-benefit incomes of single women as a group (see Table 3.2).

Although means-tested provisions had limited significance in the incomes of average recipients in most countries, the coverage measures shown in Table 3.1 show that receipt of a small amount of income from such a benefit was much more common. That table showed that more than two UK couples in five had income from means-tested benefits, as did one Norwegian couple in six and one Swedish couple in eight. In all countries the receipt of means-tested benefits was much more widespread among single aged women, including one Swedish woman in two and one Norwegian woman in four.

In five of these countries means-tested benefits function as a safety net under other, primary systems of income support, covering groups excluded by qualifying rules and/or supplementing low levels of support. Only in Australia is means-testing the primary basis of income support. Table 3.2 above showed that on average means-tested benefits form half the income of aged couples and three quarters of the income of aged single women in Australia. That table also showed that on average means-tested income also represented 18 per cent of the income of aged single women in the UK and eight per cent of the income of aged single women in Sweden. In other countries means-tested benefits represented an average of five per cent of gross income or less.

The methods and stringency of targeting of these benefits differ a good deal from country to country, and the ways in which benefit income is distributed differ accordingly. Table 3.6 shows how the total amount of income received in social assistance benefits was distributed among the members of each quintile of gross income.

Australia, relying wholly on means-tested transfers, distributed them comparatively evenly through the lower four quintiles of gross income. As the quintile distribution suggests, the function of Australian means testing was less to direct benefits to those with little other income than to withhold them from those who have a good deal. While the largest shares of benefits went to the members of the bottom three quintiles of gross income, there was a mild bias towards middle income groups in the case of both aged couples and single women. Interestingly, a somewhat similar distribution

Table 3.6

Distribution of income from means-tested transfers among quintiles of gross income for aged couples and single females

Country	Year	Quintile of gross income					Total
		Lowest	Second	Third	Fourth	Fifth	
Couples							
Australia	1985-6	22.6	24.8	26.9	17.3	8.4	100.0
(West) Germany	1984	72.2	10.7	17.1	0.0	0.0	100.0
US	1986	78.0	16.1	5.9	0.0	0.0	100.0
UK	1986	18.5	39.3	32.0	9.8	0.4	100.0
Norway	1986	25.9	25.7	17.3	23.3	7.8	100.0
Sweden	1987	72.5	25.1	1.1	1.0	0.3	100.0
Single females							
Australia	1985-6	20.3	21.6	22.2	20.2	15.7	100.0
(West) Germany	1984	32.6	30.9	13.7	9.8	13.0	100.0
US	1986	52.9	26.8	15.8	4.4	0.1	100.0
UK	1986	6.2	18.1	26.0	34.6	15.2	100.0
Norway	1986	2.3	26.0	28.9	37.6	5.3	100.0
Sweden	1987	15.4	33.8	37.4	13.4	0.0	100.0

Income units with heads aged 65 (67 in Norway) or more and living in households without other persons. Cases with negative or zero gross income have been excluded.

Source: Luxembourg Income Study database.

of means-tested benefits is shown for Norway, where means-tested benefits underpin relatively evenly distributed income from social insurance transfers. One reason for this, and for the comparatively high levels of poverty at levels above 50 per cent of median equivalent income, is the comparative immaturity of the earnings-related tier of Norwegian social insurance, with older age cohorts not yet having full entitlements.[8]

At the opposite extreme in the distribution of means-tested benefits were those countries whose primary transfer systems are most strongly earnings-related. I refer here to the US, Sweden and Germany. Among couples in these countries more than 70 per cent of means-tested benefits went to members of the lowest quintile of gross income. This pattern was less clearly shown in the case of aged single women, where because of their lower incomes the distribution of means-tested transfers included women in higher quintiles of gross income received by this group. The distribution of means-tested benefits in the UK fell between these extremes. The largest share of means-tested benefits went to aged couples and single females in the middle deciles of gross income.

Universal and selective components are intended to work together in the income support arrangements of most countries. Table 3.7 takes account of this interaction, presenting an account of the way in which social transfers as a whole are distributed across the gross income quintiles in the six countries.

As might be expected given the generally small proportions of means-tested benefits in gross income (Table 3.2), the incorporation of means-tested transfers did not make dramatic changes to the overall distribution of income from social transfers in most countries (Table 3.5). Means-tested transfers marginally increased the proportion of all transfers going to the lowest and second quintiles in most of the countries concerned. The main exception was the UK, where selective benefits were both more significant in size and more widely distributed. In the result, the shares of transfer income directed to the lowest two quintiles of couples were reduced. The broad spread of means-tested benefits in Norway was reflected in modifications of quintile shares across virtually the whole distribution. This was most marked in the case of single women.

There were several patterns in the final distribution of transfers among quintiles of gross income recipients. Australia stood alone in distributing most transfer income to the first three quartiles of gross income recipients of couples and the first four quintiles of single females, and a smaller share to the members of higher quintiles. In several of the other countries the supplementation of social insurance transfers with means-tested benefits served to even the distribution of transfers, by boosting the share of the lowest quintile of gross income recipients. In the result, benefit income was spread relatively evenly across quintiles in the UK, Norway and the United States, though the mild bias toward middle income groups in the US remained. As with social insurance transfers alone, Germany and Sweden showed strongly income-related patterns of distribution in which the members of the lowest quintiles of gross income received markedly less than their quintile share and the members of the highest quintiles markedly more.

Universality, selectivity and the redistribution of income through benefits

The previous section compared the relative importance of universal and selective benefits in the gross incomes of the aged in the six countries of the study, and examined the way in which these were distributed among quintile groups of gross income. The discussion now goes on to examine the role which universal and selective transfers play in the redistribution of income among the aged.

Table 3.7

Distribution of income from social transfers (social insurance and means-tested) among quintiles of gross income for aged couples and single females

Country	Year	Quintile of gross income					Total
		Lowest	Second	Third	Fourth	Fifth	
Couples							
Australia	1985-6	22.6	24.8	26.9	17.3	8.4	100.0
(West) Germany	1984	11.1	17.4	20.8	23.7	27.0	100.0
US	1986	15.7	20.5	23.3	21.9	18.7	100.0
UK	1986	16.0	19.0	21.0	23.3	20.7	100.0
Norway	1986	14.9	18.6	20.7	21.6	24.3	100.0
Sweden	1987	12.4	17.1	19.4	21.8	29.4	100.0
Single females							
Australia	1985-6	20.3	21.6	22.2	20.2	15.7	100.0
(West) Germany	1984	10.5	15.9	19.0	22.8	31.8	100.0
US	1986	13.5	19.5	21.3	23.6	22.2	100.0
UK	1986	18.2	21.1	21.3	20.8	18.6	100.0
Norway	1986	14.9	18.5	19.1	21.9	24.2	100.0
Sweden	1987	13.0	15.4	17.6	19.2	34.8	100.0

Income units with heads aged 65 (67 in Norway) or more and living in households without other persons. Cases with negative or zero gross income have been excluded.

Source: Luxembourg Income Study database.

The model of income used in the study, described earlier in this chapter, separates income into market and tax/transfer elements. It presents income as initially composed of wages and salaries, income from self-employment and cash property income, to which income from employment-related pensions is added to reach market income. Income from transfers may be added to market income to reach gross income, and payments of taxes and social security contributions subtracted to reach disposable or net income. The model makes it possible to identify the effects of transfers and taxes by comparing the distribution of market income 'before' transfers are received and taxes paid with the distribution of gross income and/or disposable (net) income 'afterwards'.

As has been noted, the use of this model to assess the role of transfers and taxes in redistributing income treats market income as the counterfactual, i.e.

income as it would be in the absence of welfare state intervention. In reality, however, people's expectations about taxes and transfers feed back into the workings of markets for labour and investment. This is particularly important in the case of retirement income, where workers may perceive the existence of a generous public pension scheme as reducing the need for them to seek private pensions or to save in other ways. The counterfactual problem is greater the larger the scale of public pension provision, and is particularly serious with respect to large welfare states such as Germany and Sweden. This needs to be borne in mind in the comparison of redistribution achieved under different types of pension system.

Table 3.8 below presents information about the distributions of income among aged couples and aged single women in the six countries 'before' and 'after' the operation of the tax/transfer system. While taxes and social security contributions are not generally considered in the present report, it has been noted that benefits are taxable in some countries. Mitchell (1991, pp.128-30) has shown that though less important than benefits, taxes and social security contributions play a significant role in the redistributive impact of the total transfer system. It has therefore been appropriate to include them in comparative measures of redistribution through the benefit system. The table compares the Gini coefficient measure of inequality in the distributions of income before and after the receipt of social insurance and means-tested transfers and the payment of taxes and employee contributions. The third column of the table shows the percentage reduction in inequality of market and disposable income effected by transfers and taxes in the six countries.

Among couples the greatest reduction of income inequality took place in Sweden and Germany. However, it should be borne in mind that in the LIS data sets for these two countries income from private pensions is coded with income from social insurance transfers, and these measures are not strictly comparable to those of the other countries in this respect. The smallest reduction in income inequality took place in the US. Inequality was reduced by similar proportions in Australia, the UK and Norway.[9] Among aged single women, the reduction of income inequality was greatest in the UK, Australia and Norway, but only slightly lower in Sweden and Germany. It was again least in the US. In both cases, the reduction of inequality was far smaller in the US than in any other of the five countries.

As the comparison shows, Australia's selective income support system did much less than the Swedish and German systems to reduce inequality among couples. It compares more favourably in the case of single females. Those countries whose income support systems have significant universal elements

Table 3.8
Benefits and redistribution of income

Country	Year	Gini market income	Gini disposable income	Percentage reduction of inequality
		Couples		
Australia	1985-6	.644	.245	62
(West) Germany	1984	.864	.256	70
United States	1986	.615	.339	45
United Kingdom	1986	.647	.250	61
Norway	1986	.621	.214	66
Sweden	1987	.705	.174	75
		Single females		
Australia	1985-6	.804	.199	75
(West) Germany	1984	.893	.260	71
United States	1986	.730	.363	50
United Kingdom	1986	.757	.177	77
Norway	1986	.768	.181	76
Sweden	1987	.695	.195	72

Income units with heads aged 65 (67 in Norway) or more and living in households without other persons. Cases with negative or zero gross income have been excluded.

Source: Luxembourg Income Study database.

achieved as much and more redistribution. The pattern of redistribution in the UK was very similar to that for Australia, while income support arrangements in Norway and especially Sweden did much better. German social insurance was also effective in redistributing income. The US stood alone, its pension system doing far less to reduce inequalities of income among the aged than its counterpart in any of the other five countries considered.

Redistribution and benefit expenditure

The claims made for selectivity in income support are not simply that it is more effective in directing benefits to those with fewest other resources but that it does so at lower cost to the public purse. This has been a concern with respect to both longstanding arguments about the efficiency of the market economy and more recent political pressures to contain growth in public expenditure and taxes. Thus many contemporary arguments in favour of selectivity stress the greater capacity of targeted payments to operate with comparatively low levels of social expenditure and minimal disturbance of the processes of the market economy. This section discusses evidence bearing on these arguments. In particular, it focuses on the claims that selective income support arrangements minimise welfare state intervention and that they are comparatively more efficient in the sense of achieving greater redistribution of income than universal ones per public dollar spent on them.

Income support to the aged clearly occupies a smaller share of the national economy in those countries which rely substantially on selectivity in their income support arrangements. In the mid-1980s pension expenditure in Australia was only 4.9 per cent of GDP, while pension expenditure in Sweden and Germany represented 11.2 and 11.8 per cent respectively. Shares of pension expenditure in the UK, the US and Norway were between these extremes, occupying 6.7, 7.2 and 8.0 per cent of GDP respectively (OECD, 1988a, pp.140-1). This comparison is affected by demographic differences in the proportions of the aged in the total population in the six countries. The difference stands out even more clearly when this is taken into account. When considered in relation to its share in the national economy and the share of the aged in the total population, spending on public pensions is lowest in the UK and Australia, and highest in Sweden and Germany.[10]

It is also true that selective arrangements may maximise the redistribution of income achieved at a given level of social expenditure. Some evidence for this can be seen in Table 3.9, which shows the relationship between the redistribution achieved by income support arrangements in the six countries and the importance of transfers in the gross incomes of the aged. The second column of the table reprints the percentage by which income from transfers reduced inequality in the incomes of the aged from Table 3.8 above. The third column, brought forward from Table 3.2, indicates the differing roles which transfers played in the gross incomes of the aged in these countries. Varying from 52 to 95 per cent of gross income, this measure serves as a proxy for the scale of public expenditure on income support in the six countries. The final column presents the ratio of the reduction of inequality to the share of transfer income in gross income, comparing redistribution achieved through transfers in terms of the resources devoted to them. This ratio shows the amount of redistribution achieved per dollar share of transfers in gross income.

Table 3.9
Redistribution and social expenditure on pensions

Country	Year	Percentage reduction of inequality (from Table 3.8)	Transfers as percentage of gross income (from Table 3.2)	Ratio of reduction of inequality to share of transfers in gross income
		Couples		
Australia	1985-6	62	52	1.19
(West) Germany	1984	70	87	0.80
United States	1986	45	52	0.87
United Kingdom	1986	66	67	0.91
Norway	1986	75	73	0.90
Sweden	1987	61	86	0.87
		Single females		
Australia	1985-6	75	78	0.96
(West) Germany	1984	71	95	0.75
United States	1986	50	70	0.71
United Kingdom	1986	77	81	0.95
Norway	1986	76	84	0.90
Sweden	1987	72	88	0.82

Income units with heads aged 65 (67 in Norway) or more and living in households without other persons. Cases with negative or zero gross income have been excluded.

Source: Luxembourg Income Study database.

This comparison does indeed highlight Australia's highly selective income support arrangements, which achieved greater redistribution per dollar spent than the income support system of any other of the other five countries relative to gross income.[11] The UK, whose arrangements also entail a substantial degree of selectivity, also achieved a high level of redistribution in relation to the amount spent. Interestingly, however, Norwegian arrangements achieved similar redistributive outcomes, and while these arrangements included selective elements with wide coverage they represented only a very small share of gross income on average.

The generosity of benefits

The effectiveness of income support arrangements in alleviating poverty depends not only on the capacity to direct benefits to those who need them but also on the provision of benefits at high enough levels to bring income to an adequate standard. Critics of selectivity often claim that benefit levels are higher when middle income groups share in their receipt, the corollary being that benefits which go only to the poor are poor benefits.

While benefit levels may be compared in absolute terms, the measure presented here is a relative one, comparing the benefit incomes of the aged with incomes of the working population in the same country in the same year. The benchmark used is the average take-home pay of a single worker in manufacturing industry. Table 3.10 shows the mean value of income from transfers (including both social insurance and means-tested payments) as a percentage of the average take-home pay of a manufacturing worker.[12] Since market incomes play a substantial role in the incomes of the aged in some countries, the table also shows how the disposable incomes, including both market and transfer income, of the aged compare with that of a manufacturing worker in the same country.

Looking first at mean incomes from all sources (disposable income), the average relative incomes of aged couples were highest in the US, and were comparatively high also in Norway, Sweden and Germany. The average relative incomes of aged single women were highest in Germany, and high also in the US, Norway and Sweden. The average relative incomes of both aged couples and single women were low in the UK, and were especially low in Australia.

Comparing income from social transfers, the average relative incomes of couples were lowest in Australia and in the UK and the US. They were highest in Sweden. The average income from transfers received by Australian couples was particularly low, reflecting the effect of means tests in reducing pensions below the maximum rate on account of income from investments and private pensions. The average relative levels of benefit income received by single females compared similarly except that average relative benefit incomes were higher in the UK than in the US.[13]

Average benefit levels go only part of the way to explain differences in the incidence of poverty among the aged in these six countries, shown in Table 3.4 above. Aged couples in both Sweden and Norway have comparatively high average benefit levels and low rates of poverty, while couples in the US receive comparatively low average benefits and are more commonly poor

Table 3.10

Benefit generosity: mean social transfer income and mean disposable (net) income as percentage of average take-home pay

	Year	Social transfer income		Disposable (net) income	
		C	SF	C	SF
Australia	1985-86	31.9	29.0	80.5	43.1
(West) Germany	1984	106.3	65.2	130.0	73.4
US	1986	62.1	35.3	156.0	66.2
UK	1986	60.8	43.4	101.6	55.5
Norway	1986	105.6	54.0	137.4	64.3
Sweden	1987	166.6	78.7	140.3	63.8

Income units with heads aged 65 (67 in Norway) or more and living in households without other persons. Mean benefits calculated on an aggregate share basis. Cases with negative or zero gross income have been excluded. C = couple; SF = single female.

Source: Luxembourg Income Study database; OECD (1988b), table titled 'The tax benefit position of a single person earning an amount equal to the average earnings of production workers in the manufacturing sector'.

than their counterparts in other countries. Similar patterns are found among aged single women in these countries. However, in both Australia and the UK low average benefit levels are associated with low rates of poverty, while in Germany both rates of poverty and the average level of benefit are relatively high. This pattern applies in the case of both aged couples and single females.

Conclusion

If the hallmarks of universality in income support to the aged are equality of status and common experience of government administration, the income support arrangements of Germany, Norway, Sweden and the United Kingdom might be said to be universal. The income support systems of these countries have virtually complete coverage of the age-eligible population. If the hallmark of selectivity is the conditionality of assistance upon proof of need, Australian income support stands out from those in the other five countries as uniquely selective. In actuality, the income support systems of most countries combine universal and selective elements, and means testing plays some role in the income support systems of all six countries considered here. After Australia, selectivity plays a relatively important part in the income support arrangements of the UK, where on average means-tested payments comprise 5 and 18 per cent of the gross incomes of couples and single females respectively. On this account, the UK stands out from the other four countries as having a relatively selective income support system. Following the classification proposed by the OECD (1988a), it is useful to distinguish between universality as framed by wage-related social insurance, as in Germany and the US, and universality in mixed systems where a foundation defined by 'citizenship' is supplemented by second tier of wage-related social insurance, as in the UK, Norway and Sweden.

As to whether selective arrangements are more effective than universal ones in ensuring low levels of poverty, the answers given by the present study are that 'it depends' and 'not necessarily'. It depends quite importantly on how stringently poverty is defined. When the poverty line is drawn at a low level, such as 40 per cent of median equivalent disposable income, low incidences of poverty prevailed under both selective and universal arrangements. These were higher under social insurance alone than under arrangements placing social insurance on a foundation of universal flat rate benefits. As the poverty line was drawn at higher levels, the differences in the incidence of poverty under different types of arrangements widened. The incidence of poverty under Australia's selective income support arrangements increased, as did poverty under the universal social insurance in Germany and the United States. Poverty remained low in all three countries with mixed systems of flat rate and social insurance provisions, including both the relatively selective UK and the universalist Scandinavian countries. Means-tested systems thus seem to produce a low but comprehensive safety net. Social insurance systems are more generous, but also have more gaps in coverage.

The distributive patterns associated with universal and selective income support provisions in the six countries suggest that a great variety of outcomes can be achieved under both principles. Income from universal transfers was not necessarily distributed equally in the five countries considered: while it was quite evenly distributed in relation to gross income in the UK, it was quite unevenly distributed in Germany and Sweden. As might be expected given their different weight in the various benefit systems, the distribution of means-tested transfers in relation to gross income was even more variable. Significantly, selective benefits were spread most widely in Australia and the UK, where they play larger roles in the system.

Universal and selective elements working in concert, the benefit systems of all six countries achieved substantial redistribution of income in favour of low income groups. As to whether selective arrangements are more effective than universal ones in this respect, however, the answer is again 'not necessarily'. Allowing for the overstatement of redistribution in Germany and Sweden, it appears that broadly similar levels of redistribution were achieved in five of the six countries, with only the US standing out as different and markedly less effective. However, the study did show selective arrangements as more efficient in the sense of achieving a given level of redistribution with lower levels of social expenditure. Australia and the UK clearly outperformed the other countries in this regard, though Norway was close behind.

Finally, the outcomes of income support arrangements in the six countries are a product of the interaction of the economic value of the benefits with the way they are distributed. In the evidence of the study these values were lowest in the countries making most use of selective benefits - Australia and the UK - and were particularly low in Australia where the pension system is most highly selective. They were, however, also low in the US, where social insurance provides universal coverage but private retirement income is also important. Low benefit levels contributed to poverty among the aged under both selective (Australian) and universal (US) income support systems, but the same did not appear to be true of the mixed income support arrangements of the UK.

Low benefit levels may be one reflection of lower levels of public support for social welfare expenditure in countries which rely on selective income support arrangements. The next section of this report will examine data from political opinion polls concerning attitudes to the role of government in these countries.

Notes

1   LIS data are available for both families and households. In the case of aged individuals and couples living in households with no other members, these coincide.

2   Income from private transfers and 'other' income are also included in gross income. These have little significance in the incomes of the aged in the countries concerned.

3   Because they are the main form of income support, Australian age pensions are coded as social insurance transfers in LIS. They have been recoded as means-tested transfers for the purposes of the present study.

4   The OECD scale assigns a weight of 1 to the first adult, a weight of 0.7 to each subsequent adult, and a weight of 0.5 to each child in the income unit. The Family Size scale estimates the cost of additional members of the unit as the square root of the total number of persons in the unit. It assigns a weight of 1 to the first adult, of approximately 0.4 to a second person, and approximately 0.3 to a third.

5   Using LIS data and the methodology of the UK Households Below Average Income, Whiteford and Kennedy (1995, pp.27-58) estimate that 1.0 per cent of single older people and 1.5 per cent of older persons in couples had incomes below 40 per cent of average equivalent income. They found much higher proportions of single older people (6.8 per cent) and older persons in couples (9.2) to have incomes below 50 per cent of average equivalent income, and the proportions at 60 per cent of average equivalent income (23.5 and 29.8 percent of single older people and older persons in couples respectively) far higher still. According to their measure, the proportion of aged persons living as couples having incomes below 40 per cent of average equivalent income was lower in Sweden than in the UK, but higher in Germany, Australia and the US. At 50 per cent of average equivalent income the proportion of persons living as couples was lowest in Sweden, higher in the UK and Germany, and highest in the United States and Australia. At 60 per cent of average equivalent income the proportion of individuals living as couples was lower in Sweden than in any of the other five countries included in the present study, was substantially higher in Germany, the US and the UK, and highest by far in Australia. Whiteford and Kennedy's estimates for the five countries included in the present study are all significantly higher than those shown in Table 3.4.

Percentage of individuals living as single persons and couples below 40, 50 and 60 per cent of average equivalent income, five countries, mid-1980s

Country	40 %		50 %		60 %	
	C	SF	C	SF	C	SF
Australia	5.9	6.0*	23.6*	39.4*	55.2	62.5*
Germany	3.4	4.8*	10.2	11.5*	17.3	19.1*
US	11.0	19.6*	17.4	34.0*	26.0	43.8
UK	1.5	1.0*	9.2	6.8*	29.8	23.5*
Sweden	0.3	1.8	2.0	8.2*	6.7(a)	24.2*

Note: * Exceeds sensitivity limits.
Source: Extracted from Whiteford and Kennedy, 1995, p.49.

6   Mitchell's data, drawn from the first wave of the LIS database, relate to the period around 1980 and her samples include adults of all ages and children. Saunders uses first wave LIS data from the work of Smeeding, Torrey and Rein (1988) with data from the OECD (1988a).

7   It should be noted that in the first two of these countries income from private pensions is included with income from social insurance transfers.

8   I am grateful to Joakim Palme for pointing this out to me.

9   In the case of Australia this measure might be considered to understate redistribution because it treats service pensions as private rather than public income.

10   Ratios of pension expenditure to GDP divided by the proportion of the total population aged 65 and over were UK 0.45, Australia 0.47, Norway 0.52, US 0.61, Sweden 0.66 and Germany 0.76. Population data from OECD, 1988, pp.142-3, average of 1980 and 1990.

11   The average share of transfers in gross income has been used as a proxy for social expenditure, and this is subject to errors and biases in the reporting of income. It is arguable that more income may go unreported in means-tested than universal systems.

12   The comparison worker is single and has no dependants. No equivalence scaling has been used in these calculations, hence it is not appropriate to compare the relative benefit levels of couples with those of single females.

13   This measure differs somewhat from the replacement rates conventionally used to compare the generosity of benefits in different countries, which are usually based on benefit levels at nominated points in the benefit structure. While the measure places the benefits to couples in the six countries in much the same rank order as found by Palme (1990b, p.51), for example, it shows far wider differences in level between countries. See Whiteford (1995) for a discussion of the problems involved in using replacement rates in inter-country comparisons of benefit rates.

4 Universality, selectivity and public attitudes towards income support for the aged

George Matheson

The relevance of opinion surveys

This chapter deals with the question of whether universality in income support arrangements is associated with greater levels of popular support for such expenditures than is selectivity, at least in so far as this can be gauged from public opinion surveys. In keeping with the overall focus of the report, the analysis concentrates upon popular attitudes towards state income support for the elderly, and looks at how these vary across five countries - Australia, West Germany, Great Britain, the United States and Norway - using data from the 1990 'Role of Government' wave of the *International Social Survey Programme* (Sweden was not included in this data set). In order to make sense of these variations, the data are compared with those from the previous 'Role of Government' survey in 1985, broken down by key social divisions within the five countries, and compared with the degree of measured endorsement for other aspects of social policy expenditure.

Before proceeding, however, it might be asked why such an analysis is worthwhile, given conclusions reached in Chapter 3. Certainly, it was observed that poverty among the aged in Australia and the United States appears to result from low benefit levels to a degree not encountered in the 'mixed' citizenship/insurance models of the Scandinavian countries. Nevertheless, the conclusion was inescapable that both selective and universal retirement schemes can achieve considerable redistribution of incomes, as well as poverty alleviation - at least by the most severe definition of poverty. Does not the argument for universalism contend that securing middle-class allegiance to the welfare state through giving all a stake in the system results in a greater willingness to fund social policies, thus maximising the welfare of the worst off to an extent not achievable under a (more efficient, or simply cheaper) selective regime? If so, do not the data for distributional outcomes tell the story? What is to be gained from adding the results of opinion polling?

The most obvious response is that social policy institutions are not reducible in their consequences to the purely economic aspects of social life, as opposed to the symbolic or cultural. As observed in Chapter 1, the experiences of income support recipients involve not only the securing of a minimal level of financial resources, but also perceptions of stigma, status honour and social justice. More generally, state income support arrangements do not simply allocate moneys through taxes and transfers. They also, in common with other apparatus of government, identify individuals as persons of a particular kind (worker, parent, retiree *et cetera*), define and express social values, and confer legitimacy upon some ways of life as opposed to others. Thus, to those of an egalitarian persuasion, breadth of benefit receipt and contribution *per se* is less the goal than a common experience of governance among as great a range of the citizenry as possible, in the process strengthening social solidarity and reducing social distance among citizens. Alternatively, those whose political leanings lie in a more individualist direction couch their objections to welfare universalism (or 'middle-class welfare') not just with respect to the putative economic effects of such policies, but also in terms of the independence and self-reliance they see as desirable characteristics of personality.

In other words, we are dealing with the realm of ideology, itself one of the more contested of social scientific concepts (see e.g., Eagleton, 1991). Rather than enter into the interminable debates over the 'correct' meaning of the term, it should be recognised from the outset that most senses of the word 'ideology', from a formal party *credo* to the variety of influences shaping an individual's subjectivity, are in one way or another part of the phenomenon under scrutiny. As Göran Therborn has observed:

> The actual operation of ideology in contemporary society is better illustrated by the cacophony of sounds and signs of a big city street than by the text serenely communicating with the solitary reader, or the teacher or TV-personality addressing a quiet, domesticated audience (Therborn, 1980, pp.vii-viii).

Ideology, then, represents the medium through which experiences and circumstances are translated into action. Politics, while certainly not wholly reducible to the symbolic sphere, nevertheless concerns in large part the construction and interpretation of public issues. Political actors draw upon repertoires of ideas and beliefs in explaining and justifying their decisions and actions, advocating or opposing the policies of the day, and appealing for support from the public. Considering the significance of 'public opinion' in relation to universality and selectivity in income support involves looking at the pervasiveness of ideological influences among the populace, as well as the causes and consequences of same. This leads to the next questions, namely the extent to which public opinion research can reveal anything of interest about mass ideology, and quite how it might do so.

The reputation of public opinion surveys has suffered in recent years, most notoriously in the case of the 1992 General Election in Britain, where despite polls consistently showing overwhelming support for higher taxes and social spending, the Conservatives had a clear victory on a platform advocating the opposite. This result and others like it have encouraged critics to dismiss such preferences as are expressed in surveys as an irrelevant and sanctimonious mask for the 'true' - and narrowly self-interested - desires and motivations of the public. The issue has given rise to much amusement and ridicule among conservative commentators in particular, recalling the reference by Harris and Seldon of the Institute of Economic Affairs to research on welfare attitudes as the 'priceless survey' (Harris and Seldon, 1979).

As if such a state of affairs were not sufficiently bad news for those who see the opinion poll as the authoritative *vox populi*, to be disregarded by governments at their peril, developments within the research tradition itself have been no more comforting. Indeed, in the light of the last 30 years of work in this area, one might reasonably ask if anything is left of the 'commonsense' model whereby opinion surveys retrieve the pre-existing preferences of an informed citizenry which can then be followed by a democratic and attentive political leadership.

A range of seemingly extraneous factors have been shown to influence people's responses to survey items, including choice of interviewer (Sussman, 1986), presence of reference groups (Charters and Newcomb, 1958), and even contemporaneous television news stories (Iyengar, 1991). Moreover, it is well documented that substantial differences in results can follow from variations in the specific wording and ordering of questionnaire items themselves (Mueller, 1973; Schuman and Presser, 1981; Tversky and Kahneman, 1982; Tourangeau et al., 1989). To take a well-known example, many more Americans support assistance to the 'poor' than favour similar help for 'people on welfare' (Smith, 1987).

Apparent inconsistencies among people's answers to items in the same survey have been recognised often enough, although how far these are due to the researchers' ignorance of respondents' reasoning processes remains a moot point (Burgoyne, Swift and Marshall, 1993). Perhaps most damning of all, however, has been the contention that most people simply do not *have* fixed opinions on many major political issues, which was first evidenced by response instability over time in panel data (Converse, 1964; Butler and Stokes, 1969). Attempts to argue that people do have definite and stable attitudes and that appearances to the contrary represent merely 'measurement error' (e.g., Pierce and Rose, 1974; Achen, 1975; Feldman, 1989) are faced with the problem that this 'error' typically accounts for half to three-quarters of all variance in responses (Zaller, 1992, pp.31-2). In fact, it is only among the highly educated (Converse, 1964) or more generally the politically aware (Zaller, 1992) that one finds coherent, consistent and enduring attitudinal commitments of the sort which the aforementioned naïve model of 'public opinion' would require.

Drawing all of these strands together would seem to present a bleak prognosis for the present exercise - and the preceding has not even touched upon the frequently observed lack of apparent correspondence between public opinion and policy (Smith and Wearing, 1987, 1990; Papadakis, 1992; Taylor-Gooby, 1995). Yet many of the difficulties and dilemmas outlined above presuppose a profoundly unrealistic notion of what attitude surveys are and do. A better conceptual approach to the nature and measurement of 'public opinion' would obviate many of these problems and suggest a different slant on others.

Such a perspective begins from the deceptively obvious observation that people draw upon their life experience in formulating answers to survey questions. Consequently, the meaningfulness of the responses themselves will inevitably reflect the background and circumstances of the respondents, and the perceived relevance of the topic to their lives and concerns. Thus, for those with a high level of political awareness surrounding an issue, the process may well mean the retrieval of considered and fairly settled positions. These could be attributed to formal education, such 'consciousness raising' as occurs in the course of political activity, or other direct or indirect engagement with the policy or institution under consideration. For those without any informed interest in the subject matter, on the other hand, such 'opinions' as are expressed might be more akin to an affective response or 'gut reaction' at that specific place and time to key terms or expressions in the particular question asked.

Indeed, the importance of the emotional dimension to poll responses is often overlooked. On the one hand, the recognition that attitudes have affective as well as cognitive and behavioural components is a commonplace of social psychology (Worchel and Cooper, 1983, p.43). Yet how seriously one should take the feelings of the public in mass surveys is another matter. For instance, in his review of the research literature, Zaller (1992) grants that what people express are 'real feelings', but prefers to concentrate on the role of elites, including pollsters, in shaping and representing these (1992, pp.94-5). Interestingly, this whole discussion is prefigured in Cooley's 1909 classic *Social Organization*, where democratic politics is recognised as largely an elite activity, yet 'what the masses contribute' is not ideas so much as *sentiment* (Cooley, 1962, p.135 *et seq*).

People's feelings do not exist in a vacuum, however: they reflect experiences of existing institutions and the availability of ideas in terms of which sense might be made of them. Culture, material and symbolic, provides a 'toolkit' (Swidler, 1986) with which human agency translates diffuse sensations of self-interest or sympathy or resentment into as coherent an account of things as the mind in question requires. Furthermore, while at the individual level, sentiments may fluctuate, it remains the case that at the aggregate level, consistency and gradual change are the rule, rather than the exception (Inglehart, 1985). Consequently, survey responses may be taken to reveal not only affect on the part of the respondent, but also the availability and distribution of symbolic and ideological resources within a social order. The diffusion of political thought and vocabulary through a population thus shapes access to the raw materials of political engagement, however low the 'take-up' of this might be.

Finally, the question of whether ideologies follow from other social institutions or vice versa can be avoided by the realisation that both ideologies and practices are the results of the historical conflicts of organised interests, struggles at once both instrumental and expressive. Such interests as are sufficiently successful over time can manage to institutionalise both practices, in this case systems of social provision, and the discourses in terms of which they are justified and legitimated. Given enough time, and sufficiently weak opposition, policy regimes and/or the ideologies which buttress them can become part of the taken for granted world of the community at large. A corollary of this is, to adopt a well-known phraseology, that major political actors make their own history, but they do not make it just as they please; the institutional and ideological legacy of the past limits how far governments and social movements can shape or reshape the universe of ideas to their purposes.

Opinion data from the international social survey programme

The International Social Survey Programme[1] represents a collaboration among attitude survey research teams in a number of countries, the latter having increased rapidly since the programme's inception in 1983. Its origin lay in the difficulties faced by researchers in making consistent cross-national comparisions of existing national data sets in this area. This was seen as due to variations not only in choice and wording of questions, but also in the ways in which formally identical questions were interpreted differently by various national populations. As a result, the national component surveys take the form of a standardised 'bolt-on' supplement to existing recurrent surveys of the general population (e.g., the GSS in the United States), the items being collaboratively devised in British English and thereafter translated into 'functionally equivalent' questions in the respective national languages (Davis and Jowell, 1989).

The ISSP instrument itself usually consists of a self-completion questionnaire. Of the countries in the 1990 survey included in our analyses,[2] the mode of administration was drop-off and collection in West Germany, postal survey in Australia and Norway, a combination of these techniques in Britain, and self-completion in the presence of an interviewer in the USA. Some indication of response rates can be had from the following table (Table 4.1).

The documentation for the ISSP includes comparisons of sample characteristics with other survey or census data for purposes of assessing representativeness, and readers are referred to the same (Zentralarchiv für Empirische Sozialforschung, c.1995) for details. Briefly, in so far as the checks presented there indicate, each of the national data sets would seem as reasonably representative of its national population as is typical of surveys such as these, notwithstanding the usual slight biases in favour of the prime-aged and more educated and away from blue collar workers and the unemployed.

The survey topic with which this research is concerned is the Role of Government. Specifically, the analyses cover the general public's perceptions of the responsibilities of governments with respect to aged pensions and other issues as well as how they rate aged income support as a public spending priority. While the full instrument can be found in Zentralarchiv für Empirische Sozialforschung (c1995), the questions in which we were most interested are shown in Figures 4.1 and 4.2.

Given the focus of this report, our concentration is primarily upon the 'old age pensions' item of Q. 11 and the 'Provide a decent standard of living for the old' component of Q. 18A. Nevertheless, for purposes of interpretation, it may be useful to be aware of the broader questionnaire context within which each of these two was asked. For these items, missing data were grouped with refusals, 'can't choose/don't know' responses and the like into a generic category of 'Don't know'.

Table 4.1
Response rates and sample sizes, ISSP: 1990

	Total issued	Total within scope	Valid responses	Percent response within scope
Australia	3,730	2,851	2,398	84.11
(West) Germany	5,204	5,054	2,812	55.64
Great Britain	2,293	2,210	1,197	54.16
United States	1,857	1,372	1,217	88.70
Norway	2,500	2,425	1,517	62.56

Source: ISSP, *Role of Government II*, 1990.

Background and control variables

The variables constructed for this study involve the measurement of family income, occupation/labour force status and political affiliation. Given the ISSP aim of comparability across nations, the degree to which the five countries in our study made use of different and inconsistent classifications for income and occupation data is remarkable. (In all fairness, it should be noted that the researchers involved seem well aware of this, and comparability problems have been better addressed in more recent surveys).

For Australia, Britain and the USA, occupations were recoded for this study on the basis of job titles to an approximation of the *International Standard Classification of Occupations* (ILO, 1969), such data being already available for Norway and Germany. The resultant codes were then collapsed into the major groups of this classification, and combined with data on current labour force status to give the typology employed in Figure 4.3 below. The family income data refer to annual gross income in (fairly arbitrary) categories for all countries except Germany, where only monthly net income is available. These were ranked into approximate quintiles of respondent families as presented in Table 4.4 below.

Most troublesome for the comparative researcher is inevitably the comparable classification of political parties and voting intentions. The variation in what is available for each country is striking in this regard. Not all countries included a question on 'vote last election', thus unfortunately precluding this minimally 'behavioural' measure. Instead, Germans were asked whether they 'affiliated to a certain party'; Australians and Norwegians were asked for their intention in the traditional hypothetical

83

11. Listed below are various areas of government spending. Please show whether you would like to see more or less government spending in each areas. Remember that if you say 'much more', it might require a tax increase to pay for it...

	More!!	- Spend much more
	More	- Spend more
	--	- Spend the same as now
	Less	- Spend less
	Less!!	- Spend much less
	-	- (Can't choose)

SPENDING

		More!!	More	--	Less	Less!!
a.	The environment - spend more or less?	More!!	More	--	Less	Less!!
b.	Health	More!!	More	--	Less	Less!!
c.	The police and law enforcement	More!!	More	--	Less	Less!!
d.	Education	More!!	More	--	Less	Less!!
e.	The military and defence	More!!	More	--	Less	Less!!
f.	Old age pensions	More!!	More	--	Less	Less!!
g.	Unemployment benefits	More!!	More	--	Less	Less!!
h.	Culture and the arts	More!!	More	--	Less	Less
		1	2	3	4	5

Figure 4.1   Question 11 from International Social Survey Programme questionnaire, *Role of Government:* 1990

18. On the whole do you think it should or should not be the government's responsibility to.

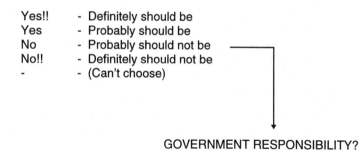

		Yes!!	Yes	No	No!!	-
a.	Provide a job for everyone who wants one	Yes!!	Yes	No	No!!	-
b.	Keep prices under control	Yes!!	Yes	No	No!!	-
c.	Provide health care for the sick	Yes!!	Yes	No	No!!	-
d.	Provide a decent standard of living for the old	Yes!!	Yes	No	No!!	-
e.	Provide industry with the help it needs to grow	Yes!!	Yes	No	No!!	-
f.	Provide a decent standard of living for the unemployed	Yes!!	Yes	No	No!!	-
g.	Reduce income differences between the rich and poor	Yes!!	Yes	No	No!!	-
h.	Give financial help to university students from low income families	Yes!!	Yes	No	No!!	-
i.	Provide decent housing for those who can't afford it	Yes!!	Yes	No	No!!	-

Figure 4.2   Question 18 from International Social Survey Programme questionnaire, *Role of Government:* 1990

mode of an 'election held tomorrow', as were the British after a number of preliminary questions regarding affiliation;[3] Americans were asked whether they saw themselves as more Democrat or Republican.

It was decided to use the ISSP team's own classification of parties onto a 'Left-Centre-Right' spectrum. It should be stressed that these designations are relative to each national polity. Thus for instance, the Greens in Australia are classified as a centre party, while *die Grünen* in Germany are assigned to the left. This measure of relativity seeks to capture the principal conflicts within each national political system, and has the advantage of avoiding explicit comparisons of party ideologies and platforms. That is, we do not have to consider such questions as whether a Norwegian conservative is to the right or the left of an American liberal. The party classifications are as follows:[4]

Australia
    Left   Labor
    Centre   Democrats, Greens, Nuclear Disarmament Party
    Right   Liberal, National

West Germany
    Left   Social Democrats, Greens
    Centre   Free Democrats
    Right   Christian Democrats

Great Britain
    Left   Labour, Greens
    Centre   Liberal, Social Democrats etc.
    Right   Conservatives, Scottish and Welsh Nationalists

United States
    Left   Democrat
    Centre   Independent
    Right   Republican

Norway
    Left   Labour, Socialist Left
    Centre   Christian Democrats, Liberal, Centre Party
    Right   Conservatives, Progress Party

In practice, Chapter 4 deals with the aforementioned criterion variables rather more than with these reclassifications, however important they may be to certain elements of the argument. The above should be enough to facilitate interpretation of the results; any further detail of methods or sample peculiarities will be introduced as and when necessary.

Basic findings: attitudes to age pensions in five countries

For the benefit of the reader who simply wants to know how much difference the type of income support arrangements makes to expressed levels of approval for age pension programs, the answer can be stated succinctly: not very much. Although, as we shall see, there are some potentially interesting minor variations among countries and these bear some relationship to the sort of welfare state prevailing, similarity of opinion generally predominates over difference. As Table 4.2 shows, people generally agree that the living standards of the aged are a responsibility of their governments and favour maintaining or expanding spending on age pensions.

The lack of opposition to the idea of state responsibility for the incomes of the old is remarkable. The only country in which even a significant minority are prepared to dissent on this issue is the United States, where nearly 12 per cent think that the government should not have such a role, and around six per cent offer no opinion. Perhaps this degree of difference might prompt speculation that individualist ideological vocabularies have been more readily available to Americans than others historically, or that living with a residualised welfare state shapes people's expectations accordingly. Yet 12 per cent is surely less than one would expect, were the former a major factor. Equally, analyses earlier in this book have shown that most of the American aged, like almost all elderly people in the countries under scrutiny, receive some form of transfer income: it is far from a wholly residual program.

Most of the other variation on this item revolves around the pattern of 'definite' as opposed to 'probable' support. Certainly, when concentrating on the former, there is some apparent relationship between universality of provision and the extent of professed strong support for state involvement. In the USA and Australia, where market income comprises a substantial proportion of the incomes of the elderly, there is the lowest incidence of definite agreement with a state responsibility in this area, while the broad-based 'mixed' systems[5] of Norway and Britain are at the other end of the scale. The German model of occupationally-based, earnings-related, yet compulsory social insurance stands between the two extremes both institutionally and attitudinally. Yet to emphasise these differences is to read a lot into the distinction between 'definitely' and 'probably'; one respondent's 'definitely should be' may indicate a genuine depth of feeling, another's an impatience with a lengthy questionnaire. Furthermore, the question remains of how far one can attribute, say, Norwegian and British strength of feeling on the subject to the experience of universal institutions as opposed to the culture and/or contingencies of national political life.

Table 4.2
Public opinion on aged income support in five countries: 1990

(a)   Should it be the government's responsibility to provide a decent standard of living for the old? (percentages)

	Definitely should be	Probably should be	Probably should not be	Definitely should not be	Don't know
Australia	37.0	56.4	5.3	0.4	0.8
(West) Germany	52.9	39.7	4.7	0.5	2.2
UK	77.9	19.1	0.9	0.4	1.8
USA	37.8	44.8	9.8	2.0	5.7
Norway	84.5	13.1	1.0	0.1	1.3

(b)   Preference for government spending on age pensions (percentages)

	Spend much more	Spend more	Spend same as now	Spend less	Spend much less	Don't know
Australia	11.6	42.6	39.8	4.3	0.6	1.0
(West) Germany	15.3	38.0	41.4	1.6	0.6	3.1
UK	32.6	50.8	13.5	0.3	0.2	2.6
USA	11.7	33.5	38.7	7.0	2.1	7.0
Norway	15.2	53.1	26.2	0.7	0.3	4.6

Source: ISSP, *Role of Government II*, 1990.

In short, regardless of the extent of selectivity or otherwise in the retirement income system, most people see the incomes of the aged as a legitimate concern of the state. What exactly this means is itself debatable, of course. Expressing general agreement with the idea that governments have responsibilities towards aged persons does not necessarily imply enthusiasm for generous state pension provision or the corresponding levels of taxes or contributions. It is quite conceivable that someone might agree with the idea that the state should aid the elderly, but believe that this would be best achieved through low general taxation and incentives for savings and private insurance.

In order to address the question of welfare universalism, it is therefore necessary to turn to the distinct, if related question of professed willingness to fund social expenditures. Again clear majorities in each country favour

88

maintaining or increasing public expenditure in this area, as indicated by Table 4.2(b). Although noticeable minorities of Americans and, to a lesser extent, Australians favour spending less on age pensions, the most apparent cross-national variation present is between Norway and the United Kingdom on the one hand, where over two-thirds of each sample favour more spending, and the remainder of the countries, where sizeable fractions of the population (around 40 per cent in each case) express contentment with the status quo. The evident British enthusiasm for spending increases is particularly noteworthy, in view of our earlier remarks. Over 80 per cent of the sample want more spending, and more than one quarter of respondents favour 'much more', despite the questionnaire's warning that this latter option 'might require a tax increase to pay for it'. It would seem far-fetched to attribute this to the rather thin universality - or indeed any other obvious structural characteristic - of the income support system. These and other data (e.g., Taylor-Gooby, 1995) suggest that there emerged a good deal of ideological opposition among the public to the Conservatives' attempted 'rolling back' of the welfare state, especially those programs with existing popularity. It might be argued that the impact of policies and programs of the decades after Beveridge on institutionalising support in the popular mind for state welfare activity was not readily undone in ten years or so. Nor can one forget the variety of opposition faced by Thatcherite ideologies, particularly given the increased salience enjoyed by equity issues as a result of a number of unpopular policies, such as, not long before this survey was fielded, the notorious 'Community Charge'.

The question arises of the stability and change in these aggregate opinion patterns. How much confidence can we have that these results are other than ephemera, triggered by the events of the day? Table 4.3 extends the analysis to look at movements over the late 1980s by comparing the previous results with those from the 1985 ISSP wave. The most striking thing about Table 4.3(a) is the degree of stability over the five year period, suggesting Ingelhart's (1985) point about the slowly moving nature of population level patterns of basic values. The only substantial shift in the pattern is a dramatic falling-off of Australian 'definitely should be' responses. While possibly attributable to the 'targeting' rhetoric of the period, it is nevertheless counterbalanced entirely by a corresponding increase in the 'probably should be' category, recalling our earlier warning about ascribing too much significance to this particular distinction. On the other hand, apparent in Table 4.3(b) is a trend away from satisfaction with prevailing expenditure towards support for increases, in West Germany, Great Britain and the United States, although this is not observed in Australia. In

Table 4.3

Public opinion on aged income support in five countries: 1985 and 1990

(a)   Should it be the government's responsibility to provide a decent standard of living for the old? (Percentages)

		Definitely should be	Probably should be	Probably should not be	Definitely should not be	Don't know
Australia	1985	59.3	32.0	3.1	0.6	5.0
	1990	37.0	56.4	5.3	0.4	0.8
	Incr. 85-90	-22.3	24.4	2.2	-0.2	-4.2
(West) Germany	1985	54.8	40.1	2.9	0.4	1.9
	1990	52.9	39.7	4.7	0.5	2.2
	Incr. 85-90	-1.9	-0.4	1.8	0.1	0.3
Great Britain	1985	77.2	19.4	1.1	0.5	1.9
	1990	77.2	20.1	0.9	0.3	1.5
	Incr. 85-90	0.0	0.7	-0.2	-0.2	-0.4
USA	1985	40.9	43.8	8.9	2.4	4.0
	1990	37.8	44.8	9.8	2.0	5.7
	Incr. 85-90	-3.1	1.0	0.9	-0.4	1.7
Norway	1985	na	na	na	na	na
	1990	84.5	13.1	1.0	0.1	1.3
	Incr. 85-90	na	na	na	na	na

(b)   Preference for government spending on age pensions (Percentages)

		Spend much more	Spend more	Spend same as now	Spend less	Spend much less	Don't know
Australia	1985	16.6	36.3	39.3	3.2	0.8	3.7
	1990	11.6	42.6	39.8	4.3	0.6	1.0
	Incr. 85-90	-5.0	6.3	0.5	1.1	-0.2	-2.7
(West) Germany	1985	10.3	34.9	48.4	3.2	0.6	2.6
	1990	15.3	38.0	41.4	1.6	0.6	3.1
	Incr. 85-90	5.0	3.1	-7.0	-1.6	0.0	0.5
Great Britain	1985	24.8	48.4	22.9	0.9	0.1	2.9
	1990	28.1	52.2	16.9	0.3	0.3	2.3
	Incr. 85-90	3.3	3.8	-6.0	-0.6	0.2	-0.6
USA	1985	12.0	28.5	39.9	9.9	2.7	7.0
	1990	11.7	33.5	38.7	7.0	2.1	7.0
	Incr. 85-90	-0.3	5.0	-1.2	-2.9	-0.6	0.0
Norway	1985	na	na	na	na	na	na
	1990	15.2	53.1	26.2	0.7	0.3	4.6
	Incr. 85-90	na	na	na	na	na	na

Source: ISSP, *Role of Government I*, 1985; *Role of Government II*, 1990.

response to any suggestion of a simple institutions-attitudes nexus, it is instructive to note that while support for more spending in Britain was high and rising in this period, the largest increase in purely percentage point terms over the five year period occurred in West Germany. Yet again, what is *not* evident in any of the five nations is any sign of a growing inclination towards reductions in expenditure.

To summarise: while there is a degree of cross-national variation in whether more or the same is preferred, hardly anyone seems to think that pensions are a bad thing, that less should be spent on them, or that retirement incomes are none of the government's business. However, it is hardly news that age pensions comprise one of the more popular categories of public spending. Not only is it consistent with previous research (Bean, 1991; Papadakis, 1992; *inter alia*), but it is intuitively plausible. What is not so obvious, perhaps, is the *absence* of substantial cross-national variation. Whether in 'individualist' America, 'corporatist' Germany or 'social-democratic' Norway, Thatcher's Britain or Hawke's Australia, most people want existing levels of provision, or more, when it comes to age pensions.

It is not hard to see how such a state of affairs could have come about. Age pensions are the longest established of social security institutions, most citizens favour and expect to benefit from them, and major conflicts over their legitimacy are things of the past. That liberal democratic states have a responsibility for the income support of the aged has become part of the taken for granted world of their citizens. It is of course the case that this apparent consensus is an historical phenomenon. While almost everyone in the industrialised countries wants either the same or more when it comes to state expenditures on the incomes of the old, this was not always the situation. Had opinion surveys been conducted in the 1890s, could anyone doubt that the present day status of age pensions as part of the furniture of routine social life would not then have been in evidence?

The conclusion of the analysis so far must be that there is no necessary or manifest connection between the nature of income support arrangements for the aged and the overall level of public commitment to the same. People seem to like support for the aged simply because they are the aged, regardless of the details of policy regimes. Does this then mean that universality and selectivity are irrelevant to citizens' evaluations of social policies, tax and transfer programs? Not necessarily, for age pensions constitute but one of the policies of the welfare state. What it does indicate is that this particular policy area, cross-national variations in response patterns are rather too minor to admit of substantial institutional explanations.

In the remainder of this chapter, two further analyses will be reported. The first involves examining the relationship between views on pension spending and position in a system of social stratification cross-nationally. The second compares attitudes to pensions in different states with opinions on other aspects of social policy.

Social differentiation and attitudes to age pensions

The discussion to this point has reported on aggregate national patterns of opinion towards government responsibility and spending with respect to income support for the aged. Yet, even in this one policy area, there remains more to the universalism question than this. Consider the situation where 50 per cent of respondents in a given country favour more age pension expenditures. From the viewpoint of comparing aggregate indicators, it presumably does not matter how this support is distributed throughout the population. Yet clearly a country in which about 50 per cent of each social stratum endorses the proposition is in a different position, politically if in no other way, from one in which nearly no-one in some social categories and virtually everyone in others expresses such a viewpoint. What is at stake, then, is the potential for social conflict over pension and other expenditures, and how this is influenced by the structure of the welfare state.

It will be recalled that the arguments of Esping-Andersen (1990) and in a slightly different sense Baldwin (1990) concern welfare universality as the expression of class alliances in social politics. Just as the formal institutions of a society limit its political possibilities, so too can one reject the notion that everyone in a national population would be equally receptive to any particular ideology which might be disseminated in the course of political mobilisation. Indeed, this is the very substance of universality/selectivity debates: does universality in social policy secure middle class backing for the welfare state? The following analyses present disaggregations of survey responses by various indicators of position in social relations and resultant command over resources in each country.

In keeping with the overall focus on incomes in this Report, the analysis begins in Table 4.4 with a breakdown of attitudes to age pension expenditure by approximate quintile of family income.[6] While it is evident from the table that the variations across nations dwarf those within, this is only to be expected given the impact of historically developed social institutions and political culture, as argued above. Nevertheless, the table also reveals variations in support and opposition by income level, and moreover, differences in this from one country to another, along broadly similar lines to what we have seen already.

Table 4.4
Preference for age pension spending by approximate income quintile: 1990
(percentages)

Quintile		Australia	(West) Germany	UK	USA	Norway
Lowest	More	62.4	61.5	87.4	55.5	71.9
	Less	3.0	2.0	0.3	4.9	0.7
	Same	33.5	32.7	7.8	30.6	21.7
	DK	1.1	3.9	4.4	9.0	5.8
Second	More	57.5	64.6	88.3	47.9	69.3
	Less	2.8	2.5	0.0	9.5	1.5
	Same	38.5	30.2	7.0	36.1	23.9
	DK	1.1	2.7	4.7	6.5	5.4
Third	More	55.6	51.4	84.5	45.7	70.1
	Less	4.8	4.1	0.7	8.2	1.3
	Same	39.0	41.3	12.8	40.3	24.2
	DK	0.5	3.3	2.0	5.8	4.4
Fourth	More	48.6	50.1	80.7	44.9	65.3
	Less	4.4	0.8	0.5	10.2	1.0
	Same	46.8	47.9	17.2	41.5	30.6
	DK	0.2	1.1	1.6	3.4	3.0
Highest	More	43.7	41.1	75.6	28.4	60.4
	Less	9.0	2.8	0.3	16.0	0.9
	Same	46.1	52.7	23.1	49.8	34.2
	DK	1.2	3.3	1.0	5.8	4.5
Total	More	53.5	53.9	83.4	44.6	67.8
	Less	4.9	2.6	0.4	9.6	1.1
	Same	40.8	40.6	13.5	39.6	26.6
	DK	0.9	2.9	2.7	6.2	4.6

Totals may differ slightly from earlier tables because of missing data.

Source: ISSP, *Role of Government II*, 1990.

Thus in Norway and Britain the only real difference as one ascends the income hierarchy consists in a shift from 'more' to 'the same', virtually no-one wanting to see less spending in this area. Even here in the two mixed insurance/assistance systems there are notable contrasts. In Britain, despite this massive amount of apparent endorsement for welfare, the proportion advocating the prevailing level of spending rather than any more does rise from seven or eight per cent in the lower income groups to almost a quarter in the highest category. In contrast, the corresponding shift from bottom to top in Norway is more gradual, even though the overall proportions favouring increasing rather than maintaining income support levels are lower than in Britain.

The differences between Norway and Britain should not be overplayed, however; almost no one in these countries wants less spending, regardless of their own income level, the only dispute being, as mentioned previously, between the same or more. Yet outside of these once or future social democracies, different patterns pertain. While Germany shows similar tendencies away from 'more' towards 'the same' with increasing income, about one person in 40 actually wishes to cut spending, although this proportion does not vary among income categories in any systematic way. The Australian data resemble to a considerable extent those for Germany, with the important exception that advocacy of spending cuts is more common and increases with income, especially near the top of the scale.

Finally, the United States stands as the odd one out among these countries, in terms of both overall levels of support/opposition and differentiation by income bracket. Comparing the highest and lowest quintiles for the US sample, the former has about half the latter's rate of support for increased spending, and more than three times its rate of endorsement for spending reductions. As the reader will recall, the Americans on the whole are also the most likely of the five national populations to favour spending cuts and least likely to want more expenditure.

Putting this together into a picture of overall attitudes and their social differentiation by income level, it may be concluded that again the United States falls at one end of the scale, with the United Kingdom and Norway at the other. Of the two countries in between, Australia is slightly more like the US, while Germany resembles its European counterparts a little more. Yet is the difference to be found in policy institutions or in the ongoing development of the political lifeworld? America and Norway differ in the extent and type of universalism in their retirement income arrangements, as well as in the expressed attitudes of their citizens with respect to this issue. However, at the risk of repetition, there is no simple relation of correspondence here. While Britain, as previously noted, makes more use of selective measures than most of the other countries, the ideological climate there in 1990 was more favourable to aged pension spending than anywhere else in this study. Briefly, a process of politicisation can have an effect in its own right.

Of course, it could be argued that welfare universalism as class politics involves not so much alliances between rich and poor as between different classes of the population defined more in terms of work and employment relations. Indeed, a program for universalism in social policy institutions is seen by some as a central element of the 'democratic class struggle' (Korpi, 1983), whereby the nineteenth century struggles among the interests of labour, land and capital have been transformed into institutionalised conflicts centred on the modern state (Stephens, 1979; Meidner, 1980; Przeworski, 1985). Aside from the more traditional accounts in terms of capital-labour antagonism, other writers proceeding from a 'new social movement' perspective have presented the welfare state as the ground for conflicts between the employed and the rest of the population, often advocating that ultimate of universal policies, the Guaranteed Minimum Income (Gorz, 1982, 1985; van Parijs, 1987).

To address a few of these concerns, Figure 4.3 presents a breakdown of preferences for more, the same or less age pension spending by labour force status and by major occupational category within the 'employed' group. It should be noted that this classification refers to the time of survey only, and thus may not be a particularly good indicator of people's situations over the life course: a clerk may or may not be *en route* to a management position, while 'retired' denotes a variety of circumstances depending on the position from which one has retired. Nevertheless, it does offer some indication of the relation between class position and attitude, and an interesting one at that. Generally speaking, variations within nations tend to be less substantial than differences in cross-national averages. Furthermore, such patterns of stratified difference as exist show a degree of formal similarity from one country to another. For instance, the self-employed and (except in Germany) farmers show the lowest rates of support for pension spending increases. Production workers more commonly favour increased spending than do managers and professionals and (everywhere but Britain) other white collar workers. By and large, those outside the active labour force are not greatly dissimilar in their responses from their employed counterparts - though not the self-employed - while the responses among the four 'non-working' categories show little variation and no apparent patterning.

One finding which, should it prove to be more than an artefact of our measurements, might bear further investigation consists of the remarkable similarity in four of the countries (the USA excepted) between the pattern of responses for the retired and that for currently-employed production workers. In Australia and Germany, about a third of both industrial workers and retirees want existing spending maintained, with around 60 per cent of

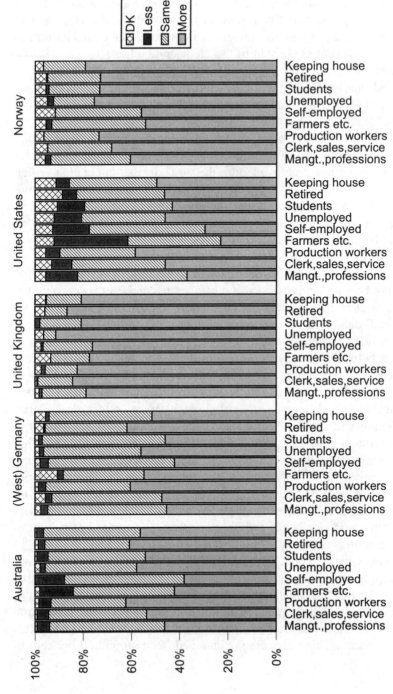

Figure 4.3 Preferences for pension spending by employment status

both categories desirous of more. Norway has corresponding proportions of around one fifth and three quarters respectively, while over 80 per cent of British respondents in these categories want more spending. Perhaps this finding could be traced simply to self-interest over the life span: the blue collar worker could be expected to be more reliant on state provision in retirement than his or her self-employed or professional counterpart. Yet there remain limits on the explanatory power of simple self-interest in this context. Certainly, the retired tend to favour pension spending, but so do the unemployed and (in some countries) housewives and students. Moreover, even sizeable proportions of the elite occupational strata favour increases in pension spending.

One final breakdown of attitudes to pensions is in order, being the most direct measurement of the degree of social division over the issue. How far do partisans of the different major political parties in each country differ when it comes to views on age pension spending? Table 4.5 addresses this question, grouping local political affiliations into the ISSP's categories of 'left', 'centre' and 'right', as defined above. As can be seen from the table, age pensions receive essentially bipartisan support in all of the countries, the only differences (once again) lying in the more/same split. In each national sample, supporters of the right-wing parties are less likely to favour increases over the status quo than are supporters of the left, with the centre parties variously more and less supportive of more spending than their more mainstream counterparts according to no particular pattern. Comparing the left and right factions in purely percentage point terms is quite interesting. In Australia, Germany and the USA, the difference between the left and right in their incidence of support for more spending is a moderate 10 to 12 percentage points, whereas in Norway, the three-quarters of Labour and other socialist voters who want to see more expenditure compare with the 70 per cent of conservatives who feel similarly.

Curiously, the biggest left-right contrast over age pension spending is to be found in the UK, where close to 90 per cent of Socialists as opposed to little more than 70 per cent of Tories choose the 'spend more' options. Even the latter, of course, is more support than the proposition gets from left wing voters in three of the other four countries. In view of our earlier discussion of the 1992 UK elections, it is tempting to ask what all the fuss was about. Most British Conservatives surveyed favoured increased age pension funding, possibly even when more taxes were involved. There is no reason to see this as ideologically inconsistent; the Conservative voter may genuinely feel for the 'deserving' poor and even be willing to assist them financially, whether due to a sense of *noblesse oblige* or a simple

Table 4.5
Preference for age pension spending by political affiliation (percentages)

		More	Same	Less	Percentage of respondents
Australia	Left	60.5	35.9	3.6	47.9
	Centre	50.4	46.5	3.1	5.9
	Right	49.1	44.3	6.6	46.1
(West) Germany	Left	61.3	37.2	1.6	56.4
	Centre	37.2	59.0	3.8	4.6
	Right	49.4	47.8	2.8	39.0
UK	Left	88.8	10.6	0.6	47.7
	Centre	88.0	12.0	0.0	9.3
	Right	71.4	27.9	0.7	43.0
USA	Left	52.5	39.2	8.3	44.9
	Centre	58.3	33.9	7.9	11.3
	Right	42.7	46.1	11.2	43.8
Norway	Left	75.5	24.3	0.2	45.4
	Centre	61.5	36.9	1.7	16.6
	Right	70.0	28.3	1.7	38.0

Source: ISSP, *Role of Government II*, 1990.

compassion for the aged and infirm. However, it is hard to see why this would translate into any automatic interest in the Labour Party, particularly given that pension and welfare issues are rarely decisive factors in people's electoral choices. People may quite sincerely favour improving age pensions, yet cast their vote according to their concerns about unemployment or general macroeconomic management, their emotional attachment to a particular party or simply force of habit.

To sum up, there are certainly (modest) variations among social strata and groups in their support for age pension spending. In general, production workers and those outside the active labour force favour age pensions more than professional/managerial workers and the self-employed, the poor more than the well off, and (unsuprisingly) leftists more than conservatives. What we are again hard-pressed to find is any sign of substantial cross-national differences in these patterns according to the prevailing system of aged income support. In the disaggregation as in the aggregates, similarity predominates over difference when it comes to cross-national popular support for the incomes of the old.

As suggested previously, the problem lies more than anything in the policy issue under consideration. People like the aged and want to help them. The same is not necessarily true of other areas of government activity. Whether universality versus selectivity might be more of an issue in other policy arenas is a question to which we now turn.

Comparisons with other policy issues

The focus of this chapter, and indeed of this book, is upon income support for the aged. By this stage, it should be apparent that this is an area of policy where opinion polls do not indicate substantial differences by policy regime. Although extension of the research into other policy areas goes beyond the scope of the present exercise, it might nonetheless prove fruitful to offer some suggestions as to where else one might look for the effects of policy universalism on public sentiment.

Table 4.6 looks at the responsibilities of governments as seen through the eyes of survey respondents in the five countries. What it shows is that the extent of cross-national variation depends on the issue under consideration. On the questions of provision of health care for the sick and, as we have seen at length, ensuring an adequate standard of living for the old, overwhelming majorities in each country see these things as legitimate state concerns.

In contrast, there are substantial differences from country to country in the proportions who view finding a job for anyone who wants one, providing a decent standard of living for the jobless, or reducing income differences between rich and poor as things the government should be doing. Furthermore, there are indications that, this time, these might be linked to institutional arrangements. Esping-Anderson's (1990) two 'liberal', market-orientated welfare states, the USA and Australia, have the lowest rates of support for all three propositions, while on the questions of full employment and income redistribution, the US actually has slender majorities *against* any government responsibility. On each of these questions, the Americans also show the highest rate of 'Don't know' responses (eight to nine per cent), presumably those with so little familiarity with the issue as to be unwilling to even hazard a guess. Conversely, in the Scandinavian full-employment welfare state that is Norway, with its credit and labour market programs and big tax-transfer system, more than two-thirds of the sample favour each of these three responsibilities, with fully 87 per cent agreeing that the

Table 4.6
Should it be the government's responsibility to...

Percentages

Country		Provide jobs for all	Control prices	Provide health care	Look after aged	Aid industry	Look after unemployed	Reduce income differences	Aid poor students	Provide low-income housing
Australia	Should be	40.4	81.9	93.1	93.4	82.8	53.3	49.7	86.5	75.3
	Should not be	56.9	16.9	6.1	5.8	14.8	42.3	47.4	11.6	20.7
	DK	2.7	1.3	0.8	0.8	2.4	4.4	2.9	1.9	4
(West) Germany	Should be	71.3	67	93.2	92.6	49	74.3	59.4	82.3	75.9
	Should not be	24.8	29.2	4.4	5.2	44.7	20.5	33.9	13.5	19.2
	DK	3.9	3.8	2.3	2.2	6.2	5.2	6.7	4.2	4.9
UK	Should be	64.3	86.9	96.9	97	89.9	79.9	72.6	90	89.5
	Should not be	30.5	9.7	0.9	1.2	6	15.7	22.3	7	6.9
	DK	5.1	3.5	2.2	1.8	4.1	4.4	5.2	3	3.6
USA	Should be	40.3	71.1	84.3	82.6	63.8	48.2	40.3	80.9	67.7
	Should not be	51.6	22.2	10.3	11.8	26.8	43	50.4	11.6	24.4
	DK	8.1	6.7	5.4	5.7	9.4	8.8	9.4	7.5	7.9
Norway	Should be	80.6	89.1	97	97.6	62.8	87.1	67.2	75.1	70.3
	Should not be	15.5	8	1.4	1.1	30.4	9	26.6	19	23.5
	DK	3.9	2.8	1.6	1.3	6.8	3.8	6.2	5.9	6.3

Source: ISSP, *Role of Government II*, 1990.

government should provide a decent standard of living for the unemployed. The rates of support for these things in Germany stand between the Australian and Norwegian situations, though somewhat closer to its European counterpart. Finally, these three items in the British survey reveal something else of interest. While the general trend of the UK responses over the nine policy areas suggests an unbridled enthusiasm for government, it is notable that only on these three does *opposition* to a government role reach double digits.

To further contextualise attitudes to aged income support, Figure 4.4 compares spending preferences with regard to age pensions with those for seven other activities of government. There is probably too much in this chart to discuss at any length here, but a few observations may be instructive. There are some cross-national similarities here as before - everyone likes spending on pensions, health, education, police and 'the environment' (whatever they understand by the latter - a good example of how an issue, indeed a symbol, permeates the public consciousness over time), while substantive fractions of the populace feel too much is being spent on defence and 'culture and the arts'. On the other hand, compare Australia's attitude to spending on unemployment benefits with that of the other countries. What, if anything, is it about the Australian unemployment relief system that encourages the deprecation of 'dole bludgers'? One intriguing possibility - and obvious prospect for further research - stems from the complete absence of any insurance element to the Australian system, uniquely among the five countries. Indeed, no similar pattern of opinion is found for the United States, which if anything rather resembles Norway on this issue. Of course, this is really a case of comparing the remarkably unlike. The actual level and type of unemployment spending as well as the public's perceptions of this status quo are very different in the two countries, well beyond differences in aged income support arrangements. Consequently, these are superficially similar evaluations of very different entities.

Because of these sorts of problems, we return for our final table to the question of state responsibility. Table 4.7 again considers differences by political affiliation, asking whether any of these other state responsibilities in the social policy field differentiates among political forces better than the age pension does. For readability, the table shows only those who think it definitely or probably is *not* the government's responsibility to do these things. It comes as no surprise that for most issues in most countries voters on the right have a higher incidence of opposition to a role for government than voters on the left; indeed, this is probably one of the defining

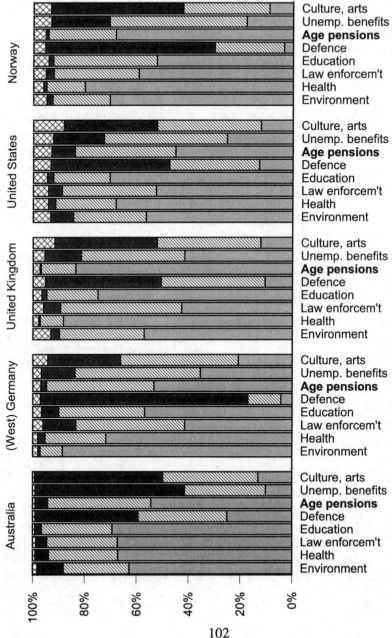

Figure 4.4 Preferences for government spending

Table 4.7

Percentages by party affiliation saying it should NOT be the responsibility of government to...

Country		Provide jobs for all	Control prices	Provide health care	Look after aged	Aid industry	Look after unemployed	Reduce income differences	Aid poor students	Provide low-income housing
Australia	Left	45.8	9.5	2.1	3.0	13.0	32.6	33.5	7.7	12.9
	Centre	58.3	14.2	6.3	5.5	19.7	43.3	36.2	7.9	16.5
	Right	68.6	24.6	9.9	8.9	15.8	52.6	63.4	16.0	29.1
(West) Germany	Left	19.6	24.7	4.3	4.0	47.2	15.0	26.6	9.4	13.2
	Centre	30.4	43.0	0.0	5.1	50.6	17.7	39.2	13.9	20.3
	Right	32.7	35.1	3.8	4.7	43.6	27.9	43.2	18.4	27.0
Great Britain	Left	21.6	7.0	0.5	0.6	6.0	9.9	11.8	4.9	1.9
	Centre	32.0	12.6	0.0	0.0	5.3	16.1	17.3	1.1	1.8
	Right	53.3	14.9	1.7	2.6	6.2	29.9	43.4	10.5	13.5
United States	Left	43.9	16.1	5.0	6.6	24.4	34.9	42.0	9.2	20.2
	Centre	46.1	14.9	7.1	12.1	26.2	41.8	41.8	10.6	16.3
	Right	61.2	30.3	16.8	16.8	29.7	51.7	61.4	14.5	30.9
Norway	Left	6.1	2.9	0.6	0.4	21.7	2.5	11.4	11.5	12.1
	Centre	14.4	4.3	1.6	1.6	39.4	11.2	21.8	19.1	23.9
	Right	28.7	17.4	2.3	1.9	37.7	14.1	47.5	25.5	36.6

Source: ISSP, *Role of Government II*, 1990.

characteristics of 'left' and 'right' in the modern world. The contrasts across policy areas, as well as national aggregates, are rather more significant. For instance, proportionately more than twice as many Republicans as Democrats think that the living standards of aged Americans are not a legitimate government concern, with rates of 16.8 and 6.6 per cent respectively. Republicans are less than one and a half times as likely as Democrats to think that income redistribution is not the government's role, but the percentages here are 61.4 and 42. Similarly, supporters of the Norwegian right-wing parties are several times more likely than those of the left to oppose a government responsibility for the unemployed, but still have only a 14.1 per cent rate of opposition to the idea, compared with rates in excess of 30 per cent for US Democrats and Australian Labor partisans.

Briefly, there do indeed appear to be sociologically and politically significant differences in the levels of support for policies within different institutional settings. The crucial policies, however, have to do with employment, unemployment and income distribution rather than support of the aged.

Conclusion

This chapter has considered the question of whether the universality of income support for the aged is reflected in the responses given to opinion surveys on the subject. It should be superfluous by now to reiterate that we found very little in this regard. To the extent that variations in national sentiments correspond to differences in welfare state structures, this is not the case for age pensions. Furthermore, it has been suggested, up to a point, why this might be so. There really is not sufficient variation in public attitudes towards aged income support arrangements for any theoretically or politically significant differences or relationships to emerge. One question still remains unaddressed, though: *why* does everyone like age pensions so much?

In fact, there are a number of possible considerations upon which people might draw in reacting to the issue of age pension expenditures. Firstly, there is simple self-interest: we all (hope to) get older, and would like to think that provisions for our retirement will be adequate. Alternatively, an explanation might remain within the bounds of self-interest, but define this more broadly to include people's sense of responsibility for their own aged relatives, whose financial upkeep they would be unable to manage but for the assistance of the state income support system. Another interpretation might emphasise respect and concern for the elderly in general as a matter of key social norms and values. Vague as this may sound, it is worth remembering that people do express favourable attitudes towards the funding of services which they do not personally use (e.g., public transport), simply because they consider it good that these things should be available (Papadakis, 1992, p.29). Yet again, considerations of fairness as reciprocity - even if not labelled so formally - might enter into people's thinking: the aged have worked and/or paid their taxes all their lives and thus are now entitled to decent living standards in their later years. Some may view the matter in terms of the rights of the citizen, and others the rights of the pension fund contributor.

The point here is not as simple as which of these explanations constitutes *the* definitive explanation for the positive responses drawn by questions on age pension spending. No doubt different respondents would draw upon differing considerations if asked to justify their choices of response, and some might well offer more than one. Indeed, the attitudes of some respondents may represent such deeply internalised, taken for granted values that they would have difficulty in verbalising *any* reason for their choices of response.

Much of the reason for the broad support enjoyed by age pension policies is undoubtedly the way in which affective, rational and habitual elements, norms, sympathy and self-interest so neatly reinforce each other. This, combined with the long established nature of aged income support systems and their resultant status as part of the taken for granted (cognitive? emotional?) world, means that the issue is one which can be expected to draw broad cross-sectional support in any of the countries under scrutiny. It also means that it is a fairly useless issue on which to test propositions about institutionally-mediated differences in mass support for social policies.

Of course, other areas of social policy, as we have seen, might be better candidates for such a test. Our only advice for the would-be researcher is to repeat our early point about the nature of opinion survey responses. All too often, research seems to proceed with an informed, calculating 'rational actor' model of the survey respondent, when what the latter does in reality may be little more than express an affective like or dislike of a policy and/or its intended beneficiaries. As Ronald Inglehart once wrote:

> The key point is that it may take a good deal of effort to put one's gut feelings into words.... In other words, one does not necessarily start with articulate, rational considerations and then derive general preferences from them; it is an interactive process in which feelings sometimes come first (Inglehart, 1985, p.101).

Notes

1   Except where otherwise indicated, the descriptions of data in this section draw upon the documentation included in the compilation *The International Social Survey Programme: Data and Documentation 1985-1992* (Zentralarchiv für Empirische Sozialforschung, c.1995).

2   We also make some limited use of the previous 'Role of Government' survey of 1985.

3   Britain in the political affiliation context denotes Great Britain; comparable data were not available for Northern Ireland.

4   Our sole adaptation of the ISSP categories consists of reclassifying the handful of communist and fascist respondents (not listed) into the main 'left' and 'right' categories respectively.

5   That is, with both flat rate and earnings-based components (see Chapter 3).

6   These 'quintiles' actually vary by about plus or minus five or six percentage points, due to the categorical nature of the income variables, but should be defined clearly enough for present purposes.

5 The Australian age pension: has targeting gone too far?

Australia's selective social security system has been held up as a model for policy directions in other countries (Castles and Mitchell, 1992; World Bank, 1994, pp.152-3). This chapter carries the discussion of universality and selectivity further, looking more closely at the nature of the tests on income and assets used to target income support to the aged. Showing what these entail in practical detail, it examines the peculiar policy challenges of means testing that aims not to restrict benefits to those with the fewest non-pension resources but to restrict pension expenditure on those having the most. Most salient among these are the intertwining of means-test arrangements with other and conflicting policy goals, the need for complex and frequently changing means-test provisions, and the tendency for means-test arrangements to be drawn into serving a wider, semi-regulatory role in the financial sector of the economy.

The incremental movement towards a universal age pension was halted in 1983, after which time tests of both income and assets have applied (Shaver, 1991). Although the rationale of restricting scarce social expenditure to those who need it most has been widely accepted, there has been continuing controversy about particular test provisions. In the early 1980s these controversies centered on the differential treatment of owner occupied housing, personal property such as furniture, jewelry or perhaps a caravan, and investment property such as stocks, bonds and real estate. The Social Security Review of the late 1980s considered the growth of private occupational superannuation and its integration with the age pension. Key issues were early retirement and the receipt of superannuation benefits as a lump sum. Their interaction with the means-tested age pension created the capacity for high income earners to arrange their affairs so as to 'double dip', claiming the age pension as well as tax-subsidised occupational pensions (Foster, 1988). New controversy arose in the early 1990s, this time

107

about means-test treatment of managed investments, and in particular of means-test assessment of nominal income from capital gains (Barber, Moon and Doolan, 1994b, pp.170-9).

Responding to a cumulative set of problems, the Government commissioned Ageing Agendas, a private consultant, to conduct an independent Strategic Review of the Pensions' Income and Assets Tests in 1994. Its terms of reference called for the examination of the rationale for income and assets testing in the context of the government's retirement income objectives; examination of the conceptual framework, design principles and operation of means test practices to minimise perceptions of intrusiveness and complexity on the part of pensioners; examination of the relationships between the income and assets tests and the tax system; to assess current provisions including the treatment of investments; and to identify options for improvement or change to the then existing income and assets tests. The Strategic Review was to consider the incomes and assets tests as they applied to all Social Security and Veterans' Affairs pensions. These issues were particularly important for the age pension in light of the increasing personal resources of the age cohorts reaching pension age.[1] The Strategic Review consulted widely with representatives of pensioner and non-pensioner groups and the finance industry as it tested policy options. It produced a discussion paper (Barber, Moon and Doolan, 1994a) and a final report (Barber, Moon and Doolan, 1994b).

The papers of the Strategic Review illuminate the way pension means testing was working in Australia in the early 1990s. Most clearly germane to the present discussion are how it was received by pensioners and by those it disqualified from the pension, how it affected economic behaviour including employment and investment activity, and what kinds of practical and policy problems it posed for government. In company with some contextual material, these papers provide a useful way of weighing the merits of selective income support in conserving public expenditure while distributing benefits to those who need them most against the social and economic costs of means testing.

The questions shaping previous sections of the book have been drawn from the case commonly made on behalf of selectivity. This section of the report takes the opposite approach, addressing questions raised about the weaknesses of selectivity. These concern the potential of means tests to affect the decisions of claimants or potential claimants in matters such as employment and investment, to undermine social cohesion, and to weaken support for the social expenditure of the welfare state.

108

Australia's 'tall poppy' test

Reference has already been made to the distinctive means tests used in Australian income support. These have been called 'tall poppies' tests because they aim to exclude claimants with the highest levels of resources rather than to limit benefits to those with the least. Reading the reports of the Strategic Review, one quickly realises the peculiar challenge which the 'tall poppy' approach to means testing poses for government. As has already been noted, means-tested benefits play a subsidiary role in the income support systems of most other countries. In consequence, means testing happens mainly to people who have little income and few assets. In Australia, however, the people who feel the cutting edge of means testing have both money and power.

This is above all clear from the kinds of income and assets to which the means test applies. Income refers not only to relatively straightforward matters of earnings, rents, interest and dividends, but also to gains or losses from the sale of bonds and shares, capital gains and income streams from structured investments. Assets refer not only to owner occupied housing but also to investment products such as units in managed funds with greatly varying investment strategies. Moreover, the relationship between claimants and property may go beyond simple ownership to include partnership and/or beneficiary interests in companies and family trusts. Such sophisticated kinds of money entail potentially sophisticated clients, or at least clients with access to sophisticated investment advice. In fact, there is a large industry catering to the market for retirement savings and all too willing to advise people about how the means test is likely to affect them. Industry representatives were among those making submissions to the Strategic Review (Barber, Moon and Doolan, 1994a; 1994b). Taken together, the class and industry groups affected by the means test make for an articulate and powerful constituency in political argument for its reform.

For government, the sophisticated interests with which means testing is concerned raises particular problems. One is the capacity of the money markets to devise investment products exploiting any loophole that appears. Another is the need to regulate the marketing of investment advice and investment products to protect small investors. While some potential pensioners have a sophisticated understanding of financial affairs, the majority undoubtedly do not and are vulnerable to the marketing of inappropriate products. Most problematic, however, is that when potentially significant resources are concerned means-test rules have implications that go beyond equity among potential claimants. In this case the means test is closely and inevitably linked with larger questions in fiscal policy. It may, for example, invite pensioners to put their money under the mattress, literally or metaphorically, when the national interest would see it invested, or cause distortions by privileging one form of savings over another. Means testing of the more usual kind rarely has to carry such burdens.

The peculiar burden of assets testing on the tall poppy model is to be seen in the framework of policy goals - what it called 'benchmarks' for means-test design - against which the Strategic Review assessed various proposals for means-test reform (Barber, Moon and Doolan, 1994b, pp.1-12). From the outset its consideration of the means test had to take account of multiple policy objectives, some of which were at least potentially in contradiction with one another.

Its terms of reference required the Review to consider the rationale for income and assets testing in the context of the government's retirement income objectives. In practice it also had to take into consideration policy commitments to the active society concept, though this is more immediately relevant to disability support and sole parents than to age pensioners. The active society concept asserts the responsibility of pensioners to take advantage of opportunities available to them to contribute to their own support through education and training, employment and optimal use of their investment resources. Retirement income policy sees the long term financial security of the aged as based on a combination of private savings including voluntary superannuation, compulsory superannuation savings through the Superannuation Guarantee Charge (SCG), and the age pension. In addition to the compulsory SCG, the policy involves tax arrangements encouraging private superannuation. Taken together, these policies define pensioners and taxpayers as partners in the provision of income support, and pension means tests as tools to be used in this context.

The retirement incomes policy involves compulsory superannuation contributions and special tax arrangements for superannuation intended to encourage retirement saving prior to retirement. The Age Pension operates in conjunction with these measures, primarily as a safety net for those who do not have the benefit of substantial superannuation or private savings.

The pensions' means test plays a major role in contributing to the overall progressivity of the retirement incomes policy by limiting the amount of pension that can be obtained by those who have benefited from superannuation tax concessions and other savings opportunities during their working lives   (Barber, Moon and Doolan, 1994b, p.3).

Through its Discussion Paper and consultations, the Strategic Review developed eleven 'benchmarks' as reference points against which means testing provisions should be measured. They were:

- that public assistance is provided in a manner which ensures social justice, by in turn ensuring that those with the least resources received the greatest measure of support;

- that those with the same or similar levels of private resources are entitled to the same level of public support;

- that the means tests operate such that a person's net final income would always be greater, as a result of self-provision, than it would have been in the absence of such effort;

- that the benefits of participating in the workforce, education or training are not reduced to the point where such participation would make little sense from the individual's point of view;

- that the means tests do not impact in such a way to influence pensioners in their choice of investments;

- that individuals are encouraged to retain and use the products of self-provision in an optimal way;

- that the structure of the pension system is affordable, within the constraints of the Government's overall fiscal strategy, and sustainable in the long term;

- that in assessing adequacy, both in terms of the entitlement and the rate of pensions, reference is made to living standards of non-pensioners within the community;

- that reforms and changes to means testing contribute to greater simplicity and clarity;

- that the means tests be flexible enough to cater to changes experienced by individuals and robust enough to provide a firm base for planning and decision making; and

- that the means tests should involve a minimal level of intrusion into the day to day lifestyles of pensioners (Barber, Moon and Doolan, 1994b, p.6).

Through its consultations the Review judged that among these eleven benchmarks the community gives greatest weight to three. These are support for social justice, ensuring that those with the least resources receive greatest support; adequacy, judged with reference to community living standards; and fairness, so that those with the same level of resources receive the same level of public support.

Even as it announced its benchmarks, the Review noted conflicts between them. The sharpest of these was between targeting for social justice on one hand and support for self-provision on the other. The Report acknowledged the inability of means testing to serve all goals equally, and stated its priority:

> It is the view of Ageing Agendas that the prime function of the means test is to target pension payments to those in most need. In a general sense, as part of that targeting function, means tests are inevitably perceived to impose a penalty on the product of self-provision. However, the income and assets tests with their exemptions, thresholds and tapered withdrawals impose a limited penalty in that, in most cases, pensioners who do self-provide are better off as a result of that self-provision, than those who have not had such opportunities.
>
> Overall, the pension system operates within a framework in which identifiable incentives are provided for self-support. However, the income and assets tests, with their primary focus on targeting, do not of themselves provide incentives. Rather, they aim to ensure that the product of self-provision is not the subject of such a penalty that individuals are deterred from acting to provide for themselves (Barber, Moon and Doolan, 1994, pp.7-8).

Thus the Review gave priority to the issues of targeting with equity with which means testing is most directly concerned, while reserving a significant but subsidiary role for issues in fostering self-provision including more general concerns of economic efficiency. It ranked classic means-testing issues to do with stigma, clarity and privacy as third in importance.

The Review addressed a number of problems in the means-test arrangements of the early 1990s. It found evidence that the provisions that applied at that time were affecting the way claimants or potential claimants were managing their resources, impinging on their responses to opportunities to provide for themselves, and distorting their choices among alternative investments. A number of particular problems surrounded the treatment of home ownership. The Review also discussed issues concerning the effect of means testing on social cohesion, particularly perceptions of means test arrangements as unfair, unduly complex and unacceptably intrusive.

The age pension means test as it operated in 1994 (Department of Social Security, 1994, pp.54-8) comprised separate tests of income and assets. For the income test, assessable income included:

- interest from bank, building society and credit union accounts;

- interest from investments such as interest bearing deposits, fixed deposits, bonds, share dividends, and family trust distributions;

- income from debentures and other loan arrangements;

- income, including capital growth, from managed investments, e.g. property trusts, friendly society bonds, and rollover investments where the owner is above age pension age;

- income from shares (including capital growth from listed shares acquired after 18 August 1992);

- gross income from earnings;

- income from businesses, including farms;

- income from rental property;

- income from boarders and lodgers;

- superannuation and overseas pensions; and

- income from immediate annuities.

Exempt income included income from social security and other benefits, board and lodging received, periodical payments from an immediate relative, and certain compensation payments.

In addition, the test took account of 'deemed income' from money held in cash or on deposit, which was assessed on any amount over $2000 for a single pensioner or $4000 for a couple. Income on such funds was assessed at four per cent or the actual interest rate, whichever was higher. The first $2000 or $4000 was assessed at the actual rate. Income was assessed at a minimum of four per cent on loans made, and on assets gifted above an annual limit, then $10 000 per year.

For the assets test, an asset was defined as any property or possession owned partly or wholly by a person, including those held outside Australia and debts owed to the person. Assessable assets included:

- cash and money in bank, building society or credit union accounts, interest bearing deposits, fixed deposits, bonds, debentures, shares, property trusts, friendly society bonds, some rollover investments and other managed investments;

- value of real estate, including holiday homes;

- value of businesses and farms, including goodwill;

- surrender value of life insurance policies;

- amounts disposed of without adequate financial return (above certain amounts);

- value of loans including interest-free loans to family trusts, members of the family, organisations, etc;

- motor vehicles, boats and caravans not used as homes;

- household contents and personal effects';

- collections for trading, investment or hobby purposes; and

- disposable, immediate or presently payable annuities.

Exempt assets included the principal home and curtilage not exceeding two hectares; the proceeds from the sale of a previous home which would be applied to the purchase of another home within 12 months; a life interest or reversionary, remainder and contingent interest not created by the pensioner; an interest in a granny flat below a certain value; an amount paid in advance for funeral expenses or a burial plot; and a number of other particular provisions.

The pension payable was the lower of the figures calculated under each of the two separate tests. Full rates in March 1994 were $318.10 per fortnight for a single person and $265.30 per fortnight for each member of a couple. Under the pensions income test, the single pension was reduced by 50 cents and the pension of each member of a couple by 25 cents for every dollar that income rose above the allowable limits. In March 1994 the allowable limits were $88 per fortnight for a single person and $152 per fortnight for the two members of a couple.

Under the pensions assets test, a pensioner could have assets of a value up to the allowable asset limit without affecting the pension. For every $1,000 over this amount, the pension was reduced by $3.00 per fortnight for a single pensioner and by $1.50 per fortnight for each member of a pensioner couple. The allowable asset limit depended on whether the pensioner was a homeowner or a non-homeowner and whether single or a member of a couple. In March 1994 these limits were $112,750 for a single homeowner, $193,250 for a single non-homeowner, $160,500 for the two members of a homeowner couple, and $241,000 for the two members of a non-homeowner couple.

Arguments about means testing for age and other pensions in Australia are played out at a secondary level in contention over access to concessions or fringe benefits attached to the pension. The value of these concessions varies considerably from one individual to another, and also from state to state and locality to locality. In 1993, eligibility for the Pensioner Concession Card which gives effect to these concessions was extended to all pensioners. It had previously been subject to a separate means test which limited its availability to pensioners receiving the full pension and having few other resources. The Government had hoped that its extension to all pensioners would address the sense of relative disadvantage expressed by pensioners then not entitled. The Pensioner Concession Card entitles the pensioner to a range of benefits. Health benefits include doctors' services billed to the government (at the doctor's discretion), assistance with the cost of pharmaceuticals, and low cost hearing and dental care. Other benefits include a telephone allowance, reduced transport fares, and reduced municipal and water rates. The holders of the card may also receive discounted prices for privately sold commodities and services such as hairdressing and movie admissions.

The Department of Social Security also provides a free Financial Information Service, located in regional offices, whose purpose is to help current and future clients to use their money to the best advantage. The service provides information about, among other matters, approaches to investments; advantages and disadvantages of different types of investments in the context of the income and assets tests; how the income and assets tests work; the availability and value of concessions under the Pensioner Concession Card; basic information on taxation issues; the availability of investment advice from outside organisations; the availability of budgeting and financial counselling services; and the effect of proposed investment arrangements on pension entitlements. The service does not recommend particular investments and does not make investments (Department of Social Security, 1994, pp.5-6).

Markets and means testing

Ageing Agendas disputed arguments presented to the Review to the effect that a targeted system in and of itself constituted a major disincentive to self-provision (Barber, Moon and Doolan, 1994b, pp.20-2). It pointed out that a home is the main asset acquired by most Australians. The exemption of the principal home is often taken for granted while it provides the pensioner with housing services, security and an asset that can be drawn on. The free areas of the income and assets tests and the generous taper rates also ensure that there is some reward for self-provision across a very broad range. Means-test disincentives had also been addressed by the extension of the Pensioner Concession Card to all pensioners, though the Review acknowledged that this had merely shifted the point at which disincentives began to be felt to the point at which pension entitlement ceases.

It found, however, that some particular provisions of the test did have disincentive effects, or created incentives affecting pensioner choices among potential investments. The most important of these were the treatment of various investment products providing income streams, the assessment of income from shares and managed investments in terms of their current rate of return, and certain savings provisions applied to investments held before the current test provisions were established. The Review also noted that the exemption of the home sometimes worked to lock pensioners into inappropriate housing (Barber, Moon and Doolan, 1994b, pp.26-7).

The report noted that means-test provisions gave more favourable treatment to investment products providing an income stream, such as superannuation pensions and purchased annuities, than to other forms of capital investment. There were a number of reasons, some historical and some technical, but preferential treatment also reflected government policy for retirement income. These investments are a preferred form of self-provision, giving a lifetime, guaranteed and indexed income in retirement, and their encouragement contributes to containing age pension outlays. Pensioners rightly felt that the means test applied to these products was more generous than that applied to other forms of investment. Private superannuation pensions were not assets tested. Moreover, income was assessed as it was received, as compared with being assessed as it accrued, and a deduction from income was allowed as representing not income but the return of capital (Barber, Moon and Doolan, 1994b, pp.19-20, 111-22). Some of these investments also attract significant tax advantages.

Though it was a source of inequity in the targeting of present day age pension expenditure, the Review regarded the favourable treatment of income streams as following legitimately from the objectives of government retirement income policy. The precise balance between these policy

116

objectives was a matter for government to decide, but the Review considered there was unresolved tension between them and that a lack of developed policy and the means-test arrangements then operating were discouraging self-provision. There were further problems in the number of different means tests applying to different income stream products. The distinctions between these were not appropriately defined, making for a high level of complexity, misinformation and distortion of investor choice. Retiree and industry groups saw policy as confused, with the Department of Social Security and the Australian Taxation Office taking different approaches to the same investment products.[2] There was a perception that means-test rules applying to income streams were likely to change again, perhaps many times, and that this created a climate of instability and unpredictability. It found inconsistencies in the reasoning applied to various types of investment products, and apparently *ad hoc* decision-making in the reconciliation of social security and taxation policy (Barber, Moon and Doolan, 1994, pp.113-16).

There was a further difficulty in distinguishing income stream products from other investments. At one extreme are investment products which are non-commutable and which provide lifetime, guaranteed, indexed pensions. At the other are accessible, highly liquid, direct investments such as cash deposits, shares and many managed investments, where all or most returns are paid as income and in which the capital can be realised at any time. There are many variations between these extremes, and at some point between them a point must be defined as limiting the favourable treatment accorded to income streams. The Review suggested there were both anomalies in the means-test treatment of apparently similar products and a lack of consensus in the community about the factors that should determine the classification of products (Barber, Moon and Doolan, 1994, p.117).

Intertwined with these problems were issues associated with the means-test treatment of capital growth. The means test then applying was based on the principle that all income should be taken into account and assessed as it accrued, reflecting the view that people should not be able to avoid the income test by electing to take their investment earnings as capital gains or deferred income. The test treated capital gains on managed investments and shares as present income, assessing them on an ongoing basis whether or not they had been realised. The same treatment was not accorded to real estate investments, where income from capital gains was not assessed until it accrued. These would, of course, be reflected in the value of assets under the asset test, but there remained an inequity in the treatment of investments of similar value but different kinds (Barber, Moon and Doolan, 1994b, pp.17-18).

This was the thorniest issue considered by the Strategic Review. Submissions argued that unrealised capital gains were not income, that they were not necessarily able to be retained, and that because of market fluctuation they could not be valued with certainty. The method of valuing them by the current rate of return was criticised on a range of technical grounds, but also for treating asset value recoveries as capital gains, as assuming that a loss or gain would be ongoing at the past rate, and as importing volatility in capital markets into pension entitlements through assessment at too frequent intervals. The Review found most of these arguments to be justified, and that it acted to deter pensioners from investments in assets of this kind and to reduce self-provision (Barber, Moon and Doolan, 1994b, pp.23-5).

In turn, the issues surrounding the treatment of capital gains were linked to those associated with savings provisions in means-test arrangements. Savings provisions have typically been enacted when changes in social security provisions would otherwise have retrospective effects. The Review noted that they contribute to stability and predictability in entitlement to the pension, and are fair in recognising that pensioners entered upon such investments on the basis of existing law. But the Review argued that certain savings provisions were also a source of unfairness because pensioners with identical investments were assessed differently only because they had purchased them on different dates. In some cases of savings provisions, the capital gain that would be assessable upon their realisation had served to lock pensioners in to investments with low or even negative returns (Barber, Moon and Doolan, 1994, pp.19, 27).

The Strategic Review also considered the effects of the income test and the high effective marginal tax rates (EMTR) arising from the interaction of means testing with income taxes on employment and other income. A single age pensioner faces an EMTR of 67 per cent over most of income range giving entitlement to a part pension (calculated from Barber, Moon and Doolan, 1994b, p.149). Noting that only two per cent of age pensioners had income from employment, this discussion was primarily concerned with sole parent and disability support pensioners. It saw the disincentive effects of high EMTRs as more significant for employment than investment income (Barber, Moon and Doolan, 1994b 155). Their impact is felt not with the first dollars of earned income but at the point where it exceeds the income disregard (in March 1994, $88 per fortnight for a single person and $152 per fortnight for the two members of a couple, Department of Social Security, 1994). The income test does not take account of the costs of employment. The Review observed that this was one factor in the concentration of pensioners' earned incomes within the pension free area, and suggested consideration of an extra disregard for earned income (Barber, Moon and

Doolan, 1994b, pp.97-100). The Review conceded that high EMTRs gave grounds for criticism with respect to self-provision for retirement, but argued that these needed to be understood in the context of the benefits accruing to retirees through superannuation tax concessions (Barber, Moon and Doolan, 1994b, p.157).

The Review considered arguments that the means testing of income made separate assets testing unnecessary and inappropriate. This had been the situation in the period 1976 to 1984, when a panel of review argued that it was a necessary feature of a 'tall poppies' test (Report of the Panel of Review, 1984). A separate assets test was necessary to provide equity to the means test, for reasons of equity and to ensure against avoidance of the income test by holding assets in non-income generating forms. The Review considered but dismissed claims that the assets-test thresholds should be lifted or the taper rates reduced (Barber, Moon and Doolan, 1994b, pp.80-1).

The treatment of owner occupied housing

Because the exemption of the family home results in different treatment of people with the same level of material resources, it is the source of substantial inequities in the targeting of the age pension. The Review noted that it creates inequities between those who have been able to acquire a substantial asset and those who have not, and treats a caravan in the same way as a house on the Sydney waterfront. It also creates inequities between those choosing to invest in a home and those saving in other forms. The Review reported, however, that:

> It proved difficult to open the subject of the exemption of the home for rational debate during the course of this Review.... At present, the pensioner community is unprepared to accept the inclusion of the principal home in a package of total assets, even with a higher threshold (Barber, Moon and Doolan, 1994b, p.82).

The separate assets-test thresholds for homeowners and non-homeowners had been adopted after a tumultuous controversy a decade earlier when it was proposed to subsume the value of the home in an overall package of allowable assets (Report of the Panel of Review, 1984; Shaver, 1991). The specification of different levels of allowable assets for homeowners and non-homeowners that has applied since that time is often referred to as the 'modified tall poppies test'.

The Review had to consider arguments about inequities and distorted investment incentives flowing from the relationship between these thresholds. Submissions pointed out that the differential, then $82,000, bore no relation to the real value of pensioners' housing, and moreover took no account of the location of the property or its market value. The differential was particularly unfair to pensioners whose homes were worth less than the difference between the thresholds. This group included farmers, pensioners living in non-urban areas, caravan and mobile home dwellers and people living in retirement villages (Barber, Moon and Doolan, 1994b, pp.82-3).

The Review also had to consider a number of particular issues associated with the treatment of owner occupied housing. One concerned the treatment of proceeds from the sale of the pensioner's home and the barrier which means testing creates to some people moving out of inappropriate housing. The sale of the house might present an opportunity for income to be generated from resources previously tied up in housing.

> When one examines the situation of pensioners in these circumstances, it can be demonstrated that they will generally enjoy higher net incomes from investing the proceeds of the sale of their housing. However, greater value is usually attached to retaining pension entitlement, with its regular, assured income, especially for those who have never invested large amounts of money before or lived on earnings from investments (Barber, Moon and Doolan, 1994b, p.124).

Means-test provisions included a twelve-month moratorium on the application of the assets test to that part of house sale proceeds which the person intends to use to purchase another home, but applied the income test to the income from such funds. The Review proposed a six-month moratorium on the application of the income test (Barber, Moon and Doolan, 1994b, pp.123-5).

The most sensitive housing question concerned the treatment of the family home when a pensioner was admitted to a nursing home. The means test provided for a two-year period during which the home remained exempt from assets testing. The Review considered that pressure to sell their homes within this period was distressing to many nursing home residents. The provision was a more significant barrier to long term wellbeing for disability support than age pensioners. The Review also found unfairness in the non-parallel treatment of people whose ill health or increasing frailty forced them to go to live with relatives. People leaving their own homes to receive community care did not benefit from the two year continuation of exemption for the family home. It recommended that the period of exemption be extended from two to three years and that the same apply to persons moving for reasons of community care (Barber, Moon and Doolan, 1994b, pp.123-30).

Stigma, social cohesion and administrative intrusion

The papers of the Strategic Review provide very little evidence that stigma or the take-up of benefits is an issue with respect to the Australian age pension. On the contrary, the issues raised in consultation and through submissions revolve almost entirely around perceptions of means-test arrangements as unfairly keeping people from the pension. This view was one motivation for submissions arguing in favour of a universal pension. A number of groups made such submissions, and two proposals were considered in some detail. The Institute of Actuaries of Australia argued that their proposal would have the advantages of encouraging self-provision and the removal of major disincentives to save, removing a source of resentment and confusion, and avoiding intrusion, while giving the aged stability, simplicity, and flexibility in the management of their financial affairs. Mary Owen offered a feminist proposal for a universal pension funded from the abolition of tax concessions for superannuation, which she argued were unfair in being geared primarily to a typical male working life. She maintained that a high flat rate pension would be more equitable than the two-tier framework of age pension and superannuation of the present retirement income policy. In contrast, a number of pensioner and older people's organisations countered with submissions to the effect that universal age pension entitlement should be extended only on the condition that existing pensioners be no worse off and that such a system be affordable and sustainable in the long term. The Review dismissed both proposals as inconsistent with its priority benchmarks of social justice, adequacy and affordability (Barber, Moon and Doolan, 1994a, pp.101-17; 1994b, pp.39-52).

Class resentments around the means test were also reflected in arguments about particular provisions of the income and assets tests. These were most evident in discussions about the treatment of investment income, particularly the use of the actual rate of return and the inclusion of capital gains, and the issues associated with the exemption of owner occupied housing. Division between country and city was reflected in discussion of the valuation of farm income and assets.

The concessions attached to receipt of the pension seem to serve as a lightning rod for the expression of resentment about the means testing of the age pension. This was one of the major subjects before the Strategic Review. In 1993 the government had responded to arguments that the means test weakened incentives to self-provision by extending the Pensioner Concession Card to all pensioners. This had required the negotiation with state governments of an agreed set of concessions and the compensation of the states for these costs. Older people whom the means test excluded from even a part pension argued that in not receiving concessions available to the majority of older people, they were being penalised for their financial independence. This was felt most strongly by those who had contributed to compulsory superannuation schemes over their working lives and had no choice but to take their superannuation as a pension rather than as a lump sum. It was suggested to the Review that access to the Pensioner Concession Card was a major motivation to arrange financial affairs to gain pension entitlement. The Review found much of this feeling confused about the nature and value of concessions. Cost and access to health services and pharmaceuticals were a major source of anxiety. In an attempt to respond to these concerns, the government had earlier offered a Seniors' Health Card to a limited group of non-pensioners who were eligible for the pension under the income test but who were cut out by the value of their assets. This card enabled those requiring prescription medicines, hearing aids or public dental treatment access to those services at a reduced rate, but did not give access to a broader range of concessions including those provided by state and local governments. Low take-up rates for this card have been attributed to resentment of the intrusion involved in the requirement to disclose information about income and assets. At the same time, the extension of concessions to all pensioners was reported to have led to the erosion of concessions in some areas. This was particularly the case where bodies such as municipal councils had made voluntary concessions in rates and charges and ceased doing so when the numbers increased. The Review heard arguments that the extension of concessions to pensioners with ample private resources had caused pensioners without other resources to suffer a decline in the real value of their pension (Barber, Moon and Doolan, 1994b, pp.136-9).

Many of the complexities of 'tall poppy' means testing will already be clear. Particular and varying rules apply to different kinds of investment, while the use of the actual rate of return method required frequent reporting of income and capital returns. The attempt to provide for the needs and circumstances of particular groups and particular events adds to these complexities. Frequent changes in policy and means-test provisions have added to these complexities. The Review's Discussion Paper noted that between 1983 and 1994 there were some 17 significant changes to income tests. Many affected only small numbers of pensioners, but their frequency was unsettling for the whole pensioner population. There were also changes to the assets test following its reinstatement in 1984. Over time, changes introduced with savings provisions introduce further layerings of complexity. In its advice to the Strategic Review the Department of Social

Security noted that change and complexity raised problems not only for pensioners but for financial advisers in the investment industry and its own staff (Barber, Moon and Doolan, 1994a, pp.27-8, 35-7). The Review concluded:

> One unequivocal outcome of the consultations has been that pensioners see the current means tests as highly complex and in many cases have argued that they result in an unacceptable level of volatility in pension entitlement. In addition, pensioners have argued that at particular times, when they move house, suffer bereavement, or are faced with entering a hursing home, that the system is inflexible and unfair.
>
> In the eyes of most pensioners, change has been a central feature of the income and assets tests during the last decade. The structure of the separate income and assets tests and the ever changing market for investment products has contributed to an environment where constant changes have had to be made for fiscal reasons and in order to maintain integrity (Barber, Moon and Doolan, 1994b, p.32).

Complexity and constant change increased pensioners' feelings of dependency and powerless in relation to the Departments of Social Security and Verans' Affairs. This was particularly so in the case of pensioners from non-English speaking backgrounds and those with poor education and/or self-confidence (Barber, Moon and Doolan, 1994b, p:33).

Although one of the objectives of the Strategic Review was to identify ways of reducing complexity and intrusiveness in the operation of means testing, the Review ranked this as less important than its priority benchmarks of support for social justice, ensuring that those with the least resources receive greatest support; adequacy, judged with reference to community living standards; and fairness, so that those with the same level of resources receive the same level of public support. It accepted a degree of complexity as inevitable for both claimants and administrators. It saw much of the system's complexity as inherent in attempts to maintain targeting with equity in a changing investment market. It offered a strategy for limiting the effects of some savings provisions, and greater effort to explain changes to pensioners as they were introduced. Its main recommendations, however, concerned the replacement of assessment of income through its current rate of return with deeming and the establishment of a pensioner financial advisory service. These are discussed in separate sections below.

Deeming of income

The Strategic Review recommended that the rate of return method be replaced with a 'deeming' approach to returns on pensioner investments. A system of this kind had operated under the 'merged means test' on income and assets that applied before 1976 and in the treatment of bank and credit union deposits at the time of the Review. The rationale for deeming was that the value of pensioners' assets is a better measure of their capacity for self-support than the income from those assets. It involves multiplying the value of a pensioner's assets by a pre-determined percentage per annum (the deeming rate) to obtain a nominal rate of earnings from those assets. The Review argued that such an approach would be simpler and clearer, give greater stability, reduce discouragement for self-provision, minimise intrusiveness and have least impact on investment choice (Barber, Moon and Doolan, 1994b, pp.53-7).

It recommended that as many investments as possible be brought within the deeming net. Exceptions should be limited to the principal home, farms, non-investment personal assets, and pensions and annuities where the capital is not accessible. Assets subject to deeming would include:

- (non-saved) managed investments and shares,
- investment real estate,
- investment personal property,
- cash investments, and
- income streams where the capital is accessible.

The Review recommended that the assets test be retained to ensure that holders of substantial property did not become eligible for pension income in periods when low rates of deeming were in use (Barber, Moon and Doolan, 1994b, pp.59-64).

The Review recommended a dual rate deeming system. This would retain the deeming system applying to bank, building society and credit union deposits, and a higher, 'general deeming rate' added for application to other investments. This should apply to assets of all kinds, including shares, managed investments, real estate, investment personal property, capital accessible income streams and cash investments other than pensioner savings accounts. The only exceptions would be the family home, non-investment personal property, farms, capital-inaccessible income stream products (which would be assessed on actual income received), and funds in pensioner savings accounts below a ceiling figure (Barber, Moon and Doolan, 1994, pp.65-70).

In discussing the application of its benchmarks to means-test design it had cautioned against expecting pensioners to pursue aggressive investment strategies. It noted that pensioners were generally investing non-renewable assets and argued that the 'optimal' return to be expected should be defined in terms of returns from relatively risk free, conservative investment (Barber, Moon and Doolan, 1994b, p.7). The general deeming rate should not attempt to replicate current rates of return in any particular sector, or overall, but should represent a rate of return which it is reasonable to expect of a pensioner retiree pursuing a reasonably conservative investment approach. The rate should vary as little as possible, and should be readily achievable by retirees in the investment marketplace (Barber, Moon and Doolan, 1994b, pp.70-4).

The Review foresaw the main problem with a shift to deeming as increased intrusiveness in the need to value assets. It suggested this could be mitigated by introducing a system of voluntary self-assessment allowing claimants choosing to employ an adviser to organise valuations and assess pension entitlement. Alternatively, it could leave applicants to make their own arrangements, with the clear understanding that the legal onus of submitting a correct valuation lay with the pensioner (Barber, Moon and Doolan, 1994b, pp.74-5).

Financial advice

As the Review put it,

> As more and more people move to supplement their retirement incomes with their own savings, the demand for appropriate retirement products and the need for information and financial advice will expand considerably... A central problem identified in this Review is that there are simply not enough truly impartial financial advisers (Barber, Moon and Doolan, 1994b, p.170).

It found that pensioners were being poorly served by private sector financial advice. It was critical of life insurance agents and the promoters of allocated pension investment products in particular. The Review considered that Government had an interest in access by retirees and pensioners to high quality investment advice. It commended the establishment of the Department of Social Security Financial Information Service and similar initiatives, and argued that further developments of this kind were needed. The Review argued that retirees and pensioners with private resources need more encouragement to seek financial advice, more guidance in the selection of financial advisers and greater access to impartial advisers who are well informed about the means test and its operation   (Barber, Moon and Doolan, 1994b, pp.170-1).

The introduction of deeming

The Government accepted many of the Review's recommendations, most importantly the introduction of an extended deeming system, to take effect from 1 July 1996.[3]   Under the new system, income from all financial investments is to be assessed by deeming. Financial investments include:

- bank, building society and credit union accounts,

- cash,

- term deposits,

- cheque accounts,

- friendly society bonds,

- managed investments,

- investments in superannuation funds, approved deposit funds and deferred annuities after age pension age,

- listed shares and securities,

- loans and debentures,

- shares in unlisted public companies, and

- gold and bullion.

Not included in financial investments are a home and its contents; cars boats and caravans; antiques, stamps or coin collections; investments in superannuation funds, approved deposit funds and deferred annuities before age pension age; standard life insurance policies; and holiday homes, farms or other real estate.

The deeming rules will be applied by adding the value of a person or couple's financial investments together. The first $30,000 of assets for a single person and $50,000 for the two members of couple will be deemed to earn an income of five per cent, with the exception that the first $2,000 (single) or $4,000 (couple) of bank deposits or cash will be assessed at the actual interest rate if less than five per cent. The amount over $30,000 (single) or $50,000 (couple) will be deemed to earn seven per cent. The actual income from these investments will not be counted except that the actual interest rate of the first $2,000 (single) or $4,000 (couple) of bank deposits or cash will be used if less than five per cent.

The exclusion from deeming of holiday homes and investment real estate was the main departure from the recommendations of the Strategic Review.

Conclusion

Chapter 1 posed the question of whether the pursuit of selectivity in income support can be taken too far. The experience of the Strategic Review suggests that the targeting of age pensions in Australia is close to the point at which it becomes counterproductive. The consequences of means testing for economic behaviour seem to be more significant than its effects on the social fabric.

Australia's selective income support in old age is generally regarded as successful in alleviating low level poverty with minimal public expenditure, though as earlier sections of the report have shown it is less successful than several other countries in providing protection against poverty at even marginally less severe standards. While the Review made adequacy one of its highest order benchmarks for considering policy options, this was not a matter for evaluation by the Review. What comes through in its Discussion Paper and Report is a perception of any relaxation of the means test as a potential threat to the adequacy of the pension.

Australia's 'tall poppies' approach compares particularly well with the means-tested arrangements of other countries in commanding widespread social acceptance among pensioners themselves. The Strategic Review consulted very widely among retiree and pensioner groups. It did not report pensioners feeling stigmatised by the status of pensioner, or reluctance to take up benefits to which they were in all likelihood entitled. On the contrary, the main effects of means tests on social cohesion lie in the resentment of 'self-funded retirees' that these arrangements are unfair, penalising them for their prudence and self-discipline. There is also some evidence that the loss of privacy in financial affairs underlies low take-up for minor benefits (see, e.g. Barber, Moon and Doolan, 1994b, p.121). These tensions drove incremental relaxation of means-test provisions during the long years of welfare state expansion (Shaver, 1991), and continue to exert political pressure in the present period. Their long history has largely accommodated them in national political culture, however, and Australians have by and large found them an acceptable price to pay for the benefits of the selective approach.

The experience of the Strategic Review does show how delicate is the balance between maintaining incentives for pensioners and potential pensioners to save, invest and take employment on the one hand and ensuring equity among claimants who do so in various ways. There is room to differ with the Review's conclusion that EMTRs of 67 per cent are not likely to diminish incentives to seek added income from sources other than employment. There is little room to doubt that the way in which the means tests define income and assets directly affects incentives to save and invest in some ways rather than others, and so distorts the working of markets for housing and financial investment.

Further direct consequences of this delicate balance are complexity and instability in means-test arrangements. Complexity flows from demands for equity in treating resources of different kinds and the need to maintain means test integrity against the exploitation of loopholes. Means test provisions have also to be reconciled with tax rules and regulations. Instability is imparted from, among other sources, the global financial economy and potentially volatile changes in interest rates and investment opportunities. Australia's attempt to value investments by their actual rate of return and the volatility this injected into pension entitlements provides a graphic illustration of such effects. Problems of this kind can be expected to remain even in the strategy of generalised deeming of income adopted following the Review.

As Ringen (1987, p.12) has pointed out, as an administrative relation between citizen and government means testing is little different from income taxation. They are very similar in intrusiveness, complexity, and potential for social division. Moreover, means testing on the Australian model has the advantage of being voluntary on the part of those citizens who seem to find it most objectionable. The discussion presented in this section is not evidence that the tall poppy test cannot be made to work. By and large Australian experience suggests that it can be. It does, however, suggest that the scope for selectivity is finite, with limits set not only by effects on economic incentives but also by the delicacy and complexity of the balancing act required.

The Strategic Review also reflected deeper problems stemming from the fact that the 'tall poppies' approach aimed at denying pension payments to those with very substantial incomes and/or assets necessarily intertwines means testing with other policies important in the management of the national economy. The most immediately relevant in Australia is retirement incomes policy, itself a primary concern of national savings policy (FitzGerald, 1993). In the result, governments face enduring difficulties in reconciling conflicts about equity with respect to incomes and assets of different kinds. Sensitive balances and compromises are required, and their achievement is made more difficult by the fact that the means test has its greatest effects among social groups with the greatest economic and political resources.

A still further consequence is the tendency for the means-testing apparatus of the social security system to become part of the regulatory structures of the financial sector, and in particular of the operation of the financial services industry. Thus means-test provisions defining the treatment of returns from investment products such as managed funds and income streams affect the kinds of products that are created and marketed. The setting of deeming rates reflects but also affects rates of interest from bank and other accounts. The regulatory effects of deeming are likely to increase the more generally it is used in means-test assessment of income. In the event, the government has been led to establish its own financial advisory services to set standards for as well as to provide independent financial advice to pensioners and would-be pensioners.

Notes

1   The Strategic Review (Barber, Moon and Doolan, 1994a, p.68) noted that while two thirds of existing pensioners received pension at the full rate, two thirds of those recently granted the pension received less than the full rate.

2   This referred to 'allocated' investment products. These are a special type of superannuation pension where the investor has an account balance from which he or she can, within minimum and maximum limits, nominate the rate of pension payment. Lump sum withdrawals can also be made. The pension may or may not be paid for the whole of the investor's lifetime, depending on the earnings the fund makes and the annual pension chosen by the purchaser (Barber, Moon and Doolan, 1994a, p.281).

3   Information in this section has been taken from Department of Social Security, 1996.

6 Conclusion

The research reported here has focused on six questions. These provide a convenient basis for summarising its findings.

What do universality and selectivity mean in practice in the income support systems of various countries?

Though most often portrayed as a two-dimensional opposition of policy choices, the contrast of universality and selectivity is more helpfully understood as multi-dimensional. Income support systems typically combine selective instruments, mainly means-tested benefits and allowances, with universal ones, commonly one or both of flat rate benefits-based and wage-related social insurance. The issues raised in the choice between selectivity and universality in income support arrangements thus concern both the nature of instruments and the balance with which they are combined in a larger system. It can thus be misleading to typify the income support systems of particular countries as simply universal or selective, or even to think of them as simply more or less universal or selective.

The research presented a twofold categorisation based on whether the income support system as a whole was of the basic, social insurance or mixed type and the average proportion of income from means-tested benefits. Categorised on this basis, Australia's income support system stood out from those of the other five countries as basic and uniquely selective. It first differed from the other five in lower coverage rates, with one quarter of aged couples and one tenth of aged single females not covered by public income support. In addition, it made much larger parts of the income of the aged subject to means test: on average more than half of the income of aged couples and single females came from selective benefits. Coverage was far more universal in all of the other five countries, with almost all citizens receiving a public benefit of some kind. These differed, however, in the

130

basis of entitlement. In Germany and the United States this was defined by membership in wage-related social insurance, with small numbers receiving a means-tested benefit to replace or supplement insurance benefits. In the social insurance countries of Germany and the United States means-tested income played a comparatively small role, accounting on average for less than 10 per cent of gross income. Selective benefits were more important in Germany than the United States. In the mixed systems of Norway, Sweden and the UK there were minimum flat rate benefits and an upper tier of social insurance, with means-tested benefits filling gaps in entitlement and supplementing benefit levels. Reliance on means-tested income support was markedly greater in the UK than in any of the other five countries. On average, means-tested benefits represented 18 per cent of the gross income of aged single women in the UK. On average these benefits made up a much smaller share of income for the aged in Norway and Sweden. They were least important in Norway.

The concept of social citizenship is often equated with universality. In this discourse universal or near-universal coverage refers to citizens having a common status as recipients of income from the public purse, as well as sharing the common experience of having one's claim assessed. In this regard, the mixed and social insurance systems of Germany, the United States, the United Kingdom, Norway and Sweden all give some foundation to social citizenship. If the criterion for citizenship includes a degree of independence of private markets, then it is limited to the 'encompassing' (Korpi and Palme, 1996) systems of Sweden and Norway.

Opinions strongly differ about whether citizenship of this kind can be conferred through means-tested benefits (see Esping-Andersen, 1990, p.48; Castles and Mitchell, 1992). It might be held that the experience of claiming a means-tested benefit contradicts and negates the inclusiveness in which citizenship inheres. In that case, there are substantial proportions of the aged in most of these countries in such circumstances, and universality of citizenship is best achieved in the social insurance countries of Germany and the United States. If the more usual view is taken, that citizenship is vitiated only by substantial dependence on means-tested income, then it is only Australia and perhaps the UK which do not qualify. A closer look at means-testing in the selective income support system with its inverted 'tall poppies' approach to selectivity (discussed in Chapter 5) suggests that means testing is not necessarily stigmatising to those who claim. Selectivity in this mode does not, however, achieve the equality of status which underlies the common identification of citizenship with universality.

Are selective income support arrangements more effective than universal ones in ensuring low levels of poverty?

The fullest definition of citizenship is the assurance of a minimum standard of wellbeing. The central claim made on behalf of selective benefits is that they are more effective than universal ones in minimising poverty because they direct resources to those who need them most. The research suggests there is some truth to this claim. At the most stringent poverty standard, poverty rates were very low in the two countries with the most selective income support systems, Australia and the UK.[1] These rates are very much higher in the social insurance countries of Germany and the US. The claim to effectiveness against poverty also applies to the mixed UK system at higher poverty thresholds.

At the same time, Australia's wholly selective income support arrangements allowed poverty rates to rise steeply at these higher thresholds. This occurs because incomes are very close to the lowest-level poverty line, and suggests some limit to the claim that selective income support is particularly effective in alleviating poverty. Poverty lines are arbitrary measures whose ultimate meaning lies in values and subjective judgements. When these lines are drawn at even slightly higher levels, Australia's selective income support system compares with others far less favourably. Nor were the safety nets of Australia and the UK the only ones which were effective in alleviating poverty among the aged. The mixed system of Sweden was equally effective, as was that of Norway at lower poverty levels.

Some interpretations of the citizenship ideal limit it to the guarantee of a minimum standard of wellbeing which is substantially independent of the market (Esping-Andersen, 1990, p.48). Viewed in this light, gaps in the safety net are greatest in Germany and the US, where social insurance arrangements afford inadequate protection to groups whose entitlements based on paid work were low. This raises issues about both minimum benefits and redistribution within social insurance schemes and the way in which entitlements accrued by a breadwinner are shared with a dependent spouse, especially after divorce or death of breadwinner. Poverty among single females in the US is especially high.

Is it true that selective income support arrangements concentrate social expenditure on those with least other income, and that in doing so achieve greater redistribution in favour of low income groups than universal arrangements? And secondly, do selective income support arrangements achieve a given level of redistribution of income more efficiently than universal ones?

The answer to the first of these questions is again 'yes, but' and 'not exclusively so'. In addressing these questions it is necessary to collapse the distinction between universality in social insurance and mixed income support systems, and to examine the distributive outcomes of selective and universal components separately as well as in combination.

The first point to be made is that the distribution of benefit income through universal transfers is greatly variable. Universal transfers were very evenly distributed among the holders of gross income in some countries, most notably the UK, while in others they gave rather larger shares of total benefit income to higher income groups. This latter pattern was most pronounced in Sweden and Germany. As is to be expected, selective transfer income was everywhere concentrated in groups having lower gross income, but the extent of this concentration also varied a good deal. Means-tested benefits were most widely distributed in countries where these benefits played a larger role in gross income, Australia and the UK, and were much more highly concentrated among those with the lowest gross income in countries where these benefits were a small part of a substantially universal system. These had the most important role in filling gaps in social insurance systems, where gaps in social insurance entitlement were not covered by universal lower tier. Norway was an exception to this pattern, however. Taken in combination, the distributive profiles of benefit income varied a good deal among the six countries. The most common pattern was for the share of each quintile in total benefit income to increase with gross income, with this pattern strongest in Germany and Sweden. With declining shares going to the highest gross income groups, Australia stands out from the other five countries.

On this evidence, it is not true that income support systems making substantial use of selectivity achieve greater redistribution in favour of low income groups than those with substantially universal arrangements. On the contrary, the reduction of income inequality was greatest in Germany and Sweden, and least in the United States. Redistribution achieved through the use of selective instruments in Australia and the UK stands between these extremes.

The research did provide support for the proposition that selective systems are more efficient than universal ones if efficient is taken to mean achieving redistribution toward low income groups and alleviating low-level poverty with minimal public expenditure. Australia's selective income support arrangements stood apart from those of the five other countries on this measure, with those of the United Kingdom also comparing favourably. It should be noted, however, that these differences were greater among couples than single women, though it is among women that selective arrangements are most important. It should also be noted that Norway's mixed income support arrangements showed themselves as comparatively efficient.

Is it the case that benefit levels are lower under selective than universal income support arrangements?

It does indeed seem that benefits earmarked for the poor are likely to be poor benefits. Average benefit income was compared with the average take-home pay of a single manufacturing worker in the same country. Benefits were especially low in Australia, where the means test serves to reduce entitlements of those claimants with private resources below the standard rate. In the UK the benefit incomes of single females, who most often depend on selective transfers, were also low. Once again, however, the relation of instruments and outcomes was not unvarying, as benefit levels were also low in the social insurance system of the United States.

Does the picture presented in surveys of political opinion suggest that there are lower levels of public support for social policy expenditure in countries with selective than universal income support arrangements?

Though the measures of support for social expenditure given by political opinion poll data do not directly translate into political support for the welfare state, they can be read as showing general ideological dispositions toward a welfare role for government. This in turn allows comparative reflection on the argument that universal benefits contribute to support for the welfare state while reliance on selective ones weakens it. In the event, we have had to conclude that we don't know. Support for social spending on the aged is similarly widespread in all five of the six countries for which such data were available, with very large majorities in all countries viewing the government as appropriately responsible for ensuring a decent standard of living for the aged. Similarly large majorities favoured spending on age pensions of at least the present level or more, with slightly greater support for increased expenditure in Norway and the UK than elsewhere. In all countries there was greater support for increased spending among lower than higher groups, and among production workers than among managers and professionals. Overall, there was no apparent relation between universality and selectivity in age pension arrangements and cross-national differences in the patterns of support for social spending on the aged. This may, however, be an artifact of the focus on public opinion data concerning support for the aged. Consideration of other policy issues suggests greater social differentiation in attitudes with respect to other policy issues. Among these, the relationship between attitudes to the unemployed and the institutional form of social programs seems most worthy of further investigation.

Can the pursuit of effectiveness and efficiency through selectivity become counterproductive?

The issues raised in the recent Strategic Review of the Pensions' Incomes and Assets Test suggest that means testing in Australia has reached the point where adverse effects of selectivity begin to be felt. The inverted, 'tall poppies' approach taken in Australia uses means testing to withhold benefit income from those with greatest private resources. This model of selectivity does seem to avoid many of the problems of stigma and poor take-up associated with means-tested benefits, or at least to do so in the Australian cultural setting. Its particular challenge is to apply means testing to groups with substantial resources of both financial and political kinds, and the process does cause resentment among the 'self-funded' retirees it excludes from receipt of the pension. The Review found that high effective marginal tax rates interfered with employment incentives. While this was not an important issue for the aged, it conflicted with active society strategies appropriate to other pensioner groups. Means-test provisions designed to foster self-provision in investment income intruded on investment choice and distorted responses to market incentives. The attempt to assess returns on investment as they accrued fed market instabilities back into pension levels. The move to assess income by 'deeming' a rate of return on investments requires the sacrifice of precision in means testing in the interests of workable compromise among inherently conflicting policy objectives. It also draws means test provisions into the regulation of capital markets. The Review found little further scope for reducing the considerable complexity of Australian means test arrangements.

Contemporary questions about the relative merits of universality and selectivity in income support arrangements are not new, but the historical context in which they are asked has changed. The debates of the 1960s and 1970s took place at the end of a long period of welfare state expansion, while those of the present time come at a moment of constraint and potential reversal. The argument may be fundamentally different in this new conjuncture.

Pierson (1994) argues that the process of retrenchment differs from that of growth in welfare state institutions. In particular, he maintains that policy

135

feedback and the existing structures of welfare state institutions play a much more important part in this process. This is because over the course of their development existing arrangements have created constituencies with interests in and attachment to them. This 'policy feedback' creates coalitions of program supporters who seek to resist cutbacks. In the result, the structure of programs shapes the possibilities for their retrenchment.

Pierson's own comparative study, of social policy in the UK and the US in the period of Thatcher and Reagan, did not show universal programs as more durable than means-tested ones. On the contrary, in both countries cuts were made to some means-tested programs but not to others. Political structures mattered, with union and left power being less important and strategic capacities of government more so. The overarching picture was of stability, with retrenchments largely limited to the margins of the welfare state. Vulnerability depended more clearly on program area, with housing and unemployment insurance bearing the greatest brunt.

Yet if Pierson's (1994, pp.6-7) account does not support the usual argument, neither does it contradict it. One would not expect large scale retrenchment in selective programs. As he points out, the weakness of selective programs was already reflected in their small size and vulnerable constituencies, and further cuts were likely to be visibly dysfunctional. Nor is it surprising that cuts were aimed at universal programs, for these were where the largest savings might be found. In the event, the universal components of aged income support were largely invulnerable during the lifetimes of the Thatcher and Reagan governments, with the significant exception of the income-related SERPS program. The most significant prospects for cutbacks to universal programs lay in the future, in tax measures implemented by the Reagan administration weakening the government's ability to finance welfare programs in the future. Finally, Pierson (1994) concludes that the relationship between retrenchment and program universality is paradoxical:

> The same features that make universal programs politically strong make them likely targets for major retrenchment efforts... knowing whether a program is targeted or universal by itself tells us relatively little about its political prospects in a period of retrenchment (Pierson, 1994, p.170).

Pierson's cases are drawn from the experience of neoliberal governments in 'liberal' welfare states (Esping-Andersen, 1990). As such, the UK and the US are more likely to represent an extreme than the generality of retrenchment and restructuring.[2] The influence of existing institutions and policy feedback may also take forms not reflected in these particular countries, and it is relevant to note that the increasing use of targeted

136

benefits is only one of many kinds of measure being implemented across a broader range of social policy regimes and income support arrangements.

Notes

1   As noted in Chapter 3, however, the poverty levels measured for the UK in the present study are subject to some qualification.

2   Nor have all 'liberal' welfare states followed the same course of retrenchment. Myles and Quadagno (1994) point out that while the United States was caught up in a 'crisis' over support for the elderly, Canadians were arguing over how to enlarge provision in that country.

Appendix: technical information

The Luxembourg Income Study (LIS) is a data bank of microdata from national income surveys recoded to be as comparable as possible. The database now contains data from approximately 15 countries for three time periods. For more information about LIS, see Smeeding, O'Higgins and Rainwater (1990).

National populations

The national populations constituted for the study comprised all income units with heads aged 65 (67 in Norway) years or more and living in households without other persons. Income figures are weighted and are based on weekly data for the United Kingdom and annual data for all other countries. Cases with negative or zero gross income have been excluded. Table A1.1 shows the sample sizes of the income survey data used.

Incomes in retirement typically vary with age, sex, and labour market status. International comparisons may be affected by inter-country differences in the demographic make up of the aged population. The following is a brief account of the extent of variations in the social and demographic characteristics of the aged populations in the six countries. For this purpose the populations of all six countries have been defined on a consistent basis, as individuals and couples with heads aged 65 or older.

Age and sex

Figure A1.1 shows distributions by age and sex of the population aged 15 and above for the six countries included in the study. While differences in the aged populations of these six countries were not large, some were substantial enough that they should be noted.

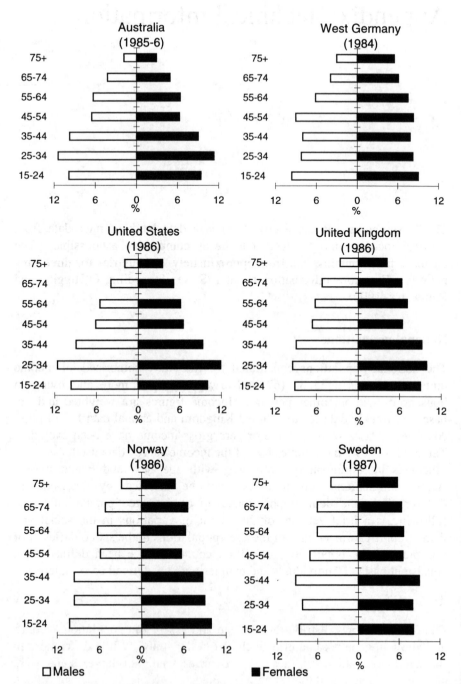

Figure A.1: Percentage of males and females in age groups (persons)
Source: Luxembourg Income Study database.

Table A1.1
Unweighted and weighted numbers of families

Sample size for each country

Country	Year	Unweighted			Weighted ('000)		
		C	SF	Total families	C	SF	Total families
Australia	1985-6	651	522	7,969	441	372	5,513
(West) Germany	1984	334	340	5,111	2,258	2,988	24,560
US	1986	872	936	12,044	6,646	7,209	93,551
UK	1986	703	675	7,156	na	na	na
Norway	1986	435	290	4,969	141	181	1,705
Sweden	1987	731	226	9,488	454	479	4,468

The youth of the Australian and US populations stands out from the comparative maturity of those of Sweden and Germany. In all six countries at least one person in every eight was aged 65 or more, but the proportions of the population in this age group varied considerably above this figure. The aged were the comparatively smallest population groups in Australia and the United States, where they represented 13.8 and 14.4 per cent of all persons (males and females together) aged 15 and over respectively. At 22.2 per cent of those 15 and over, they were a much larger part of the population in Sweden. Between these extremes, the aged accounted for 18.3, 18.5 and 19.3 per cent of those 15 and older in the UK, Germany and Norway respectively.

The comparative youth of the Australian aged also stands out in the age composition of those (all persons) aged 65 or more in the six countries, where almost two-thirds were aged 65 to 74 and only one-third were 75 or more. In Germany and Sweden 54.5 and 55.7 per cent were aged 65 to 74 respectively, and 45.6 and 44.3 were aged 75 or older. The proportion of all persons aged 65-74 in the UK, the US and Norway were 63.0, 62.3 and 60.9 per cent respectively.

Figure A1.1 also shows the balance of men and women in each age group in the six countries. There were greater proportions of women than men in the older age groups in all countries, with the difference being most pronounced in the group aged 75 and older. Differences in the proportions of men and women in the older age groups were least marked in Australia, where they reflected the comparative youth of the population as a whole, and in Sweden, where the proportions of men and women were very similar in all age groups except those aged 75 and above. The greater relative number of women than men aged 65 to 74 in Germany reflects war losses in that country.

Labour force status

Comparisons of the incomes of the aged are affected more strongly by differences in the proportions who have earnings from paid work. While majorities of the aged in all countries were not in the labour force, there were minorities of varying size who were employed on a full or part-time basis. The percentage of couples and single females in which the head of the income unit was in paid employment are shown in Table A1.2 below.

The proportion of those employed after the age of 65 ranged from fewer than one in 50 among single women in Australia to more than one in five among couples in Norway. In general, employment after age 65 was much more common among husbands than among single women. This difference was widest in Australia, and most narrow in the US. The comparatively high rates of employment in Norway were to be expected given the later age of pension eligibility in that country. For this reason, the comparative analysis of income data were restricted to single females and couples whose head was aged 67 or older. It is interesting that the share of aged couples who were employed was almost as high in the US, and was greater among aged single females in the US than in Norway. These employment patterns also to be borne in mind in the interpretation of comparative income measures for the six countries.

Table A1.2
Percentage of income unit heads aged 65+ in paid employment

Country	Couples	Single females
Australia	9.0	0.8
(West) Germany	9.0	3.3
US	16.0	7.8
UK	7.8	2.7
Sweden	8.4	1.9
Norway	17.3	6.6

Source: Luxembourg Income Study database.

Definitions of variables used in the study

Universal transfers were defined by the LIS variable 'social insurance transfers' (SOCI), which includes social retirement benefits including age, wives/carers and widows pensions, military/veterans pensions and war benefits. Sickness, accident and disability payments, child or family allowance, unemployment compensation, maternity allowances and other social insurance payments are also included in this variable but are less likely to be significant in the incomes of the aged.

Selective (means-tested) transfers were defined by the LIS variable 'means-tested income' (MEANSI), which includes means-tested cash and all near-cash benefits.

Social transfer income (SOCTRANS) is the sum of universal (SOCI) and means-tested (MEANSI) transfers.

Factor income (FI) consists of gross wages and salaries, farm and non-farm self-employment income, and cash property income.

Market income (MI) consists of factor income plus income from private and public sector pensions.

Gross income (GI) is the sum of market income and social transfer income.

Disposable (net) income (DPI) is gross income less income taxes and mandatory payroll taxes including mandatory employee contributions and mandatory contributions for self-employment.

Comparison of benefit generosity

In Table 3.10, Average Production Workers Wages (APWs) were calculated, using the aggregate share method, as (income component/APW* 100). Mean social transfer income and mean disposable income in the national currency of each country were as shown in Table A1.2, and APWs as shown in Table A1.3.

APW data were extracted from the OECD (1988b), *The Tax/Benefit Position of Production Workers 1984-87,* table titled 'The tax benefit position of a single person earning an amount equal to the average earnings of production workers in the manufacturing sector'.

Table A1.3
Mean annual social transfer income and mean disposable (net) income
in national currencies

	Year	Social transfer income		Disposable (net) income	
		C	SF	C	SF
Australia	1985-86	5,118.40	4,639.14	12,900.10	6,913.78
(West) Germany	1984	25,292.23	15,289.96	31,100.58	17,547.89
US	1986	9,197.44	5,029.72	23,314.97	9,890.86
UK	1986	360.22	2,116.20	6,429.05	3,515.68
Norway	1986	96,732.72	49,480.59	125,904.11	58,955.59
Sweden	1987	123,864.18	54,585.21	105,029.00	47,750.55

Source: Luxembourg Income Study database.

Table A1.4
Average production worker's wages

Country	Year	Take home pay and cash transfers
Australia	1985-86	16,023
(West) Germany	1984	23,916
US	1986	14,946
UK	1986	6,330
Norway	1986	91,635
Sweden	1987	74,886

References

Abel-Smith, B. and Townsend, P. (1965), *The Poor and the Poorest,* Bell and Sims: London.

Achen, Christopher H. (1975), 'Mass Political Attitudes and the Survey Response', *American Political Science Review*, 69.

Achenbaum, W. A. (1986), *Social Security: Visions and Revisions,* Cambridge University Press: Cambridge.

Alber, J. (1986), 'Germany', in Flora, P. (ed.), *Growth to Limits, The Western European Welfare States Since World War II*, Vol. 2, Walter de Gruyter: Berlin.

Alber, J. (1987), 'Germany', in Flora, P. (ed.), *Growth to Limits, The Western European Welfare States Since World War II*, Vol. 4, Walter de Gruyter: Berlin.

Alber, J. (1988), 'The West German Welfare State in Transition', in Morris, R. (ed.), *Testing the Limits of Social Welfare,* University Press of New England: Hanover.

Alber, J. (1996), 'Towards a Comparison of Recent Welfare State Developments in Germany and the United States', paper presented to the Health Policy Seminar of the Institute for Policy Studies, Yale University, New Haven, February 5, cited in Stephens, J.D., Huber, E. and Ray, L., 'The Welfare State in Hard Times', in Kitschelt, H., Lange, P., Marks, G. and Stephens, J.D. (eds), *Continuity and Change in Contemporary Capitalism*, forthcoming.

Alestalo, M. and Kuhnle, S. (1987), 'The Scandinavian Route: Economic, Social and Political Developments in Denmark, Finland, Norway, and Sweden', in Erikson, R., Hansen, E.J., Ringen, S. and Uusitalo, H. (eds), *The Scandinavian Model,* M. E. Sharpe, Inc.: Armonk, N.Y.

Anderson, B. (1983), *Imagined Communities, Reflections on the Origins and Spread of Nationalism,* Verso: London.

145

Australian Bureau of Statistics (ABS) (1991), *Superannuation Australia,* Catalogue No. 6319.0, ABS: Canberra.

Baldwin, P. (1990), *The Politics of Social Solidarity: Class Bases of the European Welfare States 1875-1975,* Cambridge University Press: Cambridge.

Barbalet, J. (1988), *Citizenship,* Open University Press: Milton Keynes.

Barber, J., Moon, G. and Doolan, S. (1994a), *Questions of Balance, A Discussion Paper,* Strategic Review of the Pensions' Income and Assets Test, Ageing Agendas, Department of Social Security: Canberra.

Barber, J., Moon, G. and Doolan, S. (1994b), *Targeting for Equity, Final Report of the Strategic Review of the Pensions Income and Assets Tests,* AGPS: Canberra.

Barry, N. (1990), *Welfare,* Open University Press: Milton Keynes.

Bean, C. (1991), 'Are Australian Attitudes to Government Different? A Comparison with Five Other Nations', in Castles, F.G. (ed.), *Australia Compared: People, Policies and Politics,* Allen and Unwin: North Sydney.

Bradshaw, J. (1993), 'Developments in Social Security Policy', in Jones, C. (ed.), *New Perspectives on the Welfare State in Europe,* Routledge: London.

Bradshaw, J., Ditch, J., Holmes, H. and Whiteford, P. (1993), *Support for Children: A Comparison of Arrangements in Fifteen Countries,* HMSO: London.

Buhmann, B., Rainwater, L., Schmaus, G. and Smeeding, T. (1988), 'Equivalence Scales, Well-being, Inequality and Poverty: Sensitivity Estimates Across Ten Countries using the Luxembourg Income Study Database', *International Review of Income and Wealth,* 34, 115-42, cited in Mitchell, D. (1991), *Income Transfers in Ten Welfare States,* Avebury: Aldershot.

Burgoyne, C., Swift, A. and Marshall, G. (1993), 'Inconsistency in Beliefs about Distributive Justice: a Cautionary Note', *Journal for the Theory of Social Behaviour,* 23.

Butler, D. and Stokes, D. (1969), *Political Change in Britain,* St Martins Press: New York.

Cappo, D. and Cass, B. (1994), 'Reworking Citizenship and Social Protection: Australia in the 1990s', paper presented to the 26th World Congress of the International Council on Social Work, July 3-7, Tampere, Finland.

146

Castles, F.G. (1985), *The Working Class and Welfare,* Allen and Unwin: Sydney.

Castles, F.G. (1994), *Is Expenditure Enough? On the Nature of the Dependent Variable in Comparative Public Policy Analysis,* Discussion Paper No. 38, Australian National University Public Policy Program, Australian National University: Canberra.

Castles, F.G. (1996), 'Leaving the Australian Labour Force: An Extended Encounter with the State', paper presented to annual meeting of ISA Research Committee 19 Poverty, Social Welfare and Social Policy, Australian National University, Canberra, 19-23 August.

Castles, F.G. and Mitchell, D. (1992), 'Identifying Welfare State Regimes: the Links Between Politics, Instruments and Outcomes', *Governance,* Vol. 5, No. 1.

Charters, W.W. and Newcomb, T. (1958), 'Some Attitudinal Effects of Experimentally Increased Salience of Group Membership', in Macoby, E., Newcomb, T. and Hartley, E. (eds), *Readings in Social Psychology,* 3rd edn, Holt, Rinehart: New York.

Converse, P. (1964), 'The Nature of Belief Systems in Mass Publics', in Apter, D. (ed.), *Ideology and Discontent,* Free Press: New York.

Cooley, C.H. (1962 [1909]), *Social Organization: A Study of the Larger Mind,* Schocken Books: New York.

Davis, J.A. and Jowell, R. (1989), 'Measuring National Differences', in Jowell, R., Witherspoon, S. and Brook, L., *British Social Attitudes - Special International Report,* 6th Report: Oxford.

Deacon, A. and Bradshaw, J. (1983), *Reserved for the Poor, The Means Test in British Social Policy,* Basil Blackwell and Martin Robertson: Oxford.

Department of Social Security (1994), *Information Handbook, A Guide to Payments and Services,* Department of Social Security: Adelaide.

Department of Social Security (1996), *Information Handbook, A Guide to Payments and Services,* Department of Social Security: Adelaide.

Dilnot, A., Disney, R., Johnson, P. and Whitehouse, E. (1994), *Pensions Policy in the UK, An Economic Analysis,* The Institute for Fiscal Studies: London.

Eagleton, Terry (1991), *Ideology: An Introduction,* Verso: London.

Eardley, T., Bradshaw, J., Ditch, J., Gough, I. and Whiteford, P. (1996), *Social Assistance in OECD Countries: Country Reports,* Research Report No. 47, Department of Social Security, HMSO: London.

Erikson, R., Hansen, E.J., Ringen, S. and Uusitalo, H. (eds) (1987), *The Scandinavian Model, Welfare States and Welfare Research,* M. E. Sharp, Inc.: Armonk, NY.

Esping-Andersen, G. (1985), *Politics Against Markets, The Social Democratic Road to Power,* Princeton University Press: Princeton, NJ.

Esping-Andersen, G. (1990), *The Three Worlds of Welfare Capitalism,* Polity: Cambridge.

Esping-Andersen, G. and Korpi, W. (1987), 'From Poor Relief to Institutional Welfare States: the Development of Scandinavian Social Policy', in Erikson, R., Hansen, E.J., Ringen, S. and Uusitalo, H. (eds), *The Scandinavian Model,* M. E. Sharpe, Inc.: Armonk, N.Y.

Feldman, Stanley (1989), 'Reliability and Stability of Policy Positions: Evidence from a Five-Wave Panel', *Political Analysis,* Vol. 1.

FitzGerald, V.W. (1993), *National Savings, A Report to the Treasurer,* AGPS: Canberra.

Flora, P. (1986), 'Introduction', in Flora, P. (ed.), *Growth to Limits, The Western European Welfare States Since World War II,* Walter de Gruyter: Berlin.

Förster, M. (1993), 'Comparing Poverty in 13 OECD Countries - Traditional and Synthetic Approaches', Working Paper No. 100, Luxembourg Income Study, CEPS/INSTEAD: Luxembourg.

Foster, C. (1988), *Towards a National Retirement Incomes Policy,* Issues Paper No. 6, Social Security Review, Department of Social Security: Canberra.

Friedman, M. (1962), *Capitalism and Freedom,* University of Chicago Press: Chicago.

Friedmann, R.R. (1987), 'Welfare States: a Summary of Trends', in Friedmann, R.R., Gilbert, Neil and Sherer, Moshe (eds), *Modern Welfare States, A Comparative View of Trends and Prospects,* Wheatsheaf Books: Brighton, Sussex.

Garfinkel, I. (1982), 'Introduction', in Garfinkel, I. (ed.), *Income-Tested Transfer Programs, The Case For and Against,* Academic Press: New York.

George, V. and Wilding, P. (1985), *Ideology and Social Welfare,* Routledge and Kegan Paul: London.

Gilbert, G. (1966), *The Evolution of National Insurance in Great Britain,* Michael Joseph: London.

Gilbert, N. (1988), 'Changing Structures for the Delivery of Social Benefits in the United States', in Morris, R. (ed.), *Testing the Limits of Social Welfare,* University Press of New England: Hanover.

Glazer, N. (1988), *The Limits of Social Policy,* Harvard University Press: Cambridge, MA.

Gorz, André (1982), *Farewell to the Working Class,* Pluto Press: London.

Gorz, André (1985), *Paths to Paradise. On the Liberation from Work,* Pluto Press: London and Sydney.

Guillemard, A.M. (ed.) (1983), *Old Age and the Welfare State,* Sage: London.

Harris, J. (1981), 'Some Aspects of Social Policy in Britain During the Second World War', in Mommsen, W.J. (ed.), *The Emergence of the Welfare State in Britain and Germany,* Croom Helm: London, cited in Deacon, A. and Bradshaw, J. (1983), *Reserved for the Poor, The Means Test in British Social Policy,* Basil Blackwell and Martin Robertson: Oxford.

Harris, R. and Seldon, A. (1979), *Overruled on Welfare,* Institute for Economic Affairs: London.

Hedstrom, P. and Ringen, S. (1990), 'Age and Income in Contemporary Society', in Smeeding, T., O'Higgins, M. and Rainwater, L. (eds), *Poverty, Inequality and Income Distribution in Comparative Perspective,* Harvester Wheatsheaf: New York.

Henderson, R.F. (1977), 'Criteria for Welfare: Needs or Earnings?' *Australian Journal of Social Issues,* Vol. 12, No. 2.

Hernes, H. M. (1987), *Welfare State and Woman Power,* Norwegian University Press: Oslo.

Hill, M. (1990), *Social Security Policy in Britain,* Edward Elgar: Aldershot.

Hippe, J. and Pedersen, A.W. (1988), 'For Lang og Tro Tjeneste. Pensjoner i Arbeidsmarkedet', FAFO-report No. 084: Oslo.

Inglehart, Ronald (1985), 'Aggregate Stability and Individual-level Flux in Mass Belief Systems: the Level of Analysis Paradox', *American Political Science Review,* Vol. 79.

Inter-departmental Committee on Social Insurance and Allied Services (1942), *Social Insurance and Allied Services,* Report by Sir William Beveridge, Cmd. 6404, HMSO: London.

International Labour Office (ILO) (1969), *International Standard Classification of Occupations,* ILO: Geneva.

Iyengar, Shanto (1991) *Is Anyone Responsible?,* University of Chicago Press: Chicago.

Jencks, C. (1982), 'Discussion' [of Coleman, J., 'Income Testing and Social Cohesion'], in Garfinkel, I. (ed.), *Income-Tested Transfer Programs, The Case For and Against,* Academic Press: New York.

Kamerman, S.B. and Kahn, A.J. (1987), 'Universalism and Income Testing in Family Policy: New Perspectives on an Old Debate', *Social Work,* Vol. 32, No. 3.

Kewley, T.H. (1973), *Social Security in Australia, 1900-1972,* Sydney University Press: Sydney.

Klein, R. (1993), 'O'Goffe's Tale', in Jones, C. (ed.), *New Perspectives on the Welfare State in Europe,* Routledge: New York.

Kohl, Juergen K. (1992), 'The Public/Private Mix in the Income Package of the Elderly, a Comparative Study', paper presented to conference, Social Security 50 Years After Beveridge, University of York, England, September.

Korpi, W. (1983), *The Social Democratic Class Struggle,* Routledge and Kegan Paul: London.

Korpi, W. and Palme. J. (1996), 'The Paradox of Redistribution and the Strategy of Equality: On the Role of Welfare State Institutions for Inequality and Poverty in the Western Countries', paper presented to annual meeting of ISA Research Committee 19, Poverty, Social Welfare and Social Policy, Australian National University, Canberra, 19-23 August 1996.

Kuhnle, S. (1986), 'Norway', in Flora, P. (ed.), *Growth to Limits, The Western European Welfare States Since World War II,* Vol. 1, Walter de Gruyter: Berlin.

Kuhnle, S. (1987), 'Norway', in Flora, P. (ed.), *Growth to Limits, The Western European welfare states since World War II,* Vol. 4, Walter de Gruyter: Berlin.

Lawrence, J. (1986), 'Comparative Study of Social Policy: Conceptual and Methodological Issues', *The International Journal of Sociology and Social Policy,* Vol. 6, No. 3.

Le Grand, J. (1982), *The Strategy of Equality, Redistribution on the Social Sciences,* Allen and Unwin: London.

McCallum, J. (1991), 'The Three Historic Phases of Australian Superannuation', *Superfunds,* 142, October.

Marshall, T. H. (1963), 'Citizenship and Social Class', in Marshall, T.H., *Sociology at the Crossroads,* Heinemann: London.

Meidner, R. (1980), 'Our Concept of the Third Way: Some Remarks on the Socio-political Tenets of the Swedish Labour Movement', *Economic and Industrial Democracy,* Vol. 1, No. 3.

Mishra, R. (1981), *Society and Social Policy,* 2nd edn, Humanities Press: Atlantic Highlands, NJ.

Mitchell, D. (1991), *Income Transfers in Ten Welfare States,* Avebury: Aldershot.

Morris, R. (1988), 'Changing Patterns of Public Social Welfare Policy in Nine Countries, 1975-1986: Predicting Future Trends', in Morris, R. (ed.), *Testing the Limits of Social Welfare, International Perspectives on Policy Changes in Nine Countries,* University Press of New England for Brandeis University Press: Hanover.

Mueller, John (1973), *War, Presidents and Public Opinion,* Wiley: New York.

Myles, J. (1989), *Old Age in the Welfare State, The Political Economy of Public Pensions,* rev. edn, The University Press of Kansas: Lawrence, KA.

Myles, J. and Quadagno, J. (1994), 'The Politics of Income Security for the Elderly in North America: Founding Cleavages and Unresolved Conflicts', in Marmor, T., Smeeding, T.M. and Greene, V.L. (eds), *Economic Security and Intergenerational Justice, A Look at North America,* The Urban Institute Press: Washington, D.C.

Myles, J. and Quadagno, J. (1997), 'Recent Trends in Public Pension Reform: a Comparative View', in Banting, K. and Broadway, R. (eds), *Reform of Retirement Income Policy: International and Canadian Perspectives,* School of Policy Studies, Queens University: Kingston, Ontario, Canada.

Nielsen, F. v. N. (1991), 'The Politics of Aging in Scandinavian Countries', in Myles, J. and Quadagno, J. (eds), *States, Labor Markets and the Future of Old Age Policy,* Temple University Press: Philadelphia, PA.

Nordic Social-Statistical Committee (1990), *Social Security in the Nordic Countries, Scope, Expenditure and Financing 1987,* Nordic Statistical Secretariat: Copenhagen.

Offe, C. (1984), *Contradictions of the Welfare State,* MIT Press: Cambridge, MA.

Olson, S. (1986), 'Sweden', in Flora, P. (ed.), *Growth to Limits, The Western European Welfare States Since World War II,* Vol. 1, Walter de Gruyter: Berlin.

Olsson, S. (1987), 'Sweden', in Flora, P. (ed.), *Growth to Limits, The Western European Welfare States Since World War II,* Vol. 4, Walter de Gruyter: Berlin.

Olsson, S. (1988), 'Decentralization and Privatization: Strategies Against a Welfare Backlash in Sweden', in Morris, R. (ed.), *Testing the Limits of Social Welfare,* University Press of New England: Hanover.

Organisation for Economic Co-operation and Development (OECD) (1988a), *Reforming Public Pensions,* OECD Social Policy Studies No. 5, OECD: Paris.

Organisation for Economic Co-operation and Development (OECD) (1988b), *The Tax/Benefit Position of Production Workers 1984-1987,* OECD: Paris.

Organisation for Economic Co-operation and Development (OECD) (1994), *New Orientations for Social Policy,* OECD Social Policy Studies No. 12, OECD: Paris.

151

Orloff, A. S. (1993), *The Politics of Pensions, A Comparative Analysis of Britain, Canada, and the United States, 1880-1940*, University of Wisconsin Press: Madison, WI.

Øverbye, E. (1992), *Public or Private Pensions? Pensions and Pension Politics in the Nordic Countries*, Working Paper No. 38, Institute of Industrial Relations, University of California at Berkeley: Berkeley, CA.

Palme, J. (1990a), 'Models of Old Age Oensions', in Ware, A. and Goodin, R.E. (eds), *Needs and Welfare*, Sage: London.

Palme, J. (1990b), *Pension Rights in Welfare Capitalism, The Development of Old-age Pensions in 18 Countries 1930 to 1985*, Swedish Institute for Social Research, Stockholm University: Stockholm.

Pampel, F.C. and Williamson, J.B. (1989), *Age, Class Politics and the Welfare State*, Cambridge University Press: Cambridge.

Papadakis, Elim (1992), 'Public Opinion, Public Policy and the Welfare State', *Political Studies*, Vol. 40.

Parry, R. (1987), 'United Kingdom', in Flora, P. (ed.), *Growth to Limits, The Western European Welfare States Since World War II*, Vol. 4, Walter de Gruyter: Berlin.

Perry, R. (1986), 'United Kingdom', in Flora, P. (ed.), *Growth to Limits, The Western European Welfare States Since World War II*, Vol. 2, Walter de Gruyter: Berlin.

Pestieau, P. (1992), 'The Distribution of Private Pension Benefits: How Fair is It?', in Organisation for Economic Co-operation and Development, *Private Pensions and Public Policy*, Social Policy Studies No. 9, OECD: Paris.

Pierce, J.C. and Rose, D. (1974), 'Nonattitudes and American Public Opinion: Examination of a Thesis', *American Political Science Review*, Vol. 68.

Pierson, C. (1991), *Beyond the Welfare State?*, Polity: Cambridge.

Pierson, P. (1994), *Dismantling the Welfare State? Reagan, Thatcher, and the Politics of Retrenchment*, Cambridge University Press: Cambridge.

Pixley, J. (1993), *Citizenship and Employment, Investigating Post-industrial Options*, Cambridge University Press: Cambridge.

Probert, B. (1995), 'Basic Income and Socially Useful Work', *Just Policy*, Vol. 4, September.

Przeworski, Adam (1985), *Capitalism and Social Democracy*, Cambridge University Press: Cambridge.

Quadagno, J. (1988), *The Transformation of Old Age Security*, University of Chicago Press: Chicago.

Quadagno, J. (1991), 'Interest-group Politics and the Future of US Social Security', in Myles, J. and Quadagno, J. (eds), *States, Labor Markets and the Future of Old Age Policy*, Temple University Press: Philadelphia, PA.

Rainwater, L. (1982), 'Stigma in Income-tested Programs', in Garfinkel, I. (ed.), *Income-Tested Transfer Programs, The Case For and Against*, Academic Press: New York.

Rainwater, L. (1992), 'The Poor in Comparative Perspective', paper prepared for the International Research Conference on Poverty and Distribution, Central Bureau of Statistics, Oslo, November 16-17, cited in Whiteford, P. and Kennedy, S. (1995), *Incomes and Living Standards of Older People, A Comparative Analysis*, Research Report No. 34, Department of Social Security, HMSO: London.

Report of the Panel of Review of the Proposed Income and Assets Test (1984), Gruen, F., Chairman, Department of Social Security: Canberra.

Rimlinger, G.V. (1971), *Welfare Policy and Industrialization in Europe, America, and Russia*, John Wiley and Sons, Inc.: New York.

Ringen, S. (1987), *The Possibility of Politics*, Clarendon Press: Oxford.

Saunders, P. (1991), 'Selectivity and Targeting in Income Support: The Australian Experience', *Journal of Social Policy*, Vol. 20, No. 3.

Saunders, P. (1994), *Welfare and Inequality, National and International Perspectives on the Australian Welfare State*, Cambridge University Press: Cambridge.

Schmähl, W. (1993), 'The "1992 Reform" of Public Pensions in Germany: Main Elements and Some Effects', *Journal of European Social Policy*, Vol. 3, No. 1.

Schuman, H. and Presser, S. (1981), *Questions and Answers in Attitude Surveys*, Wiley: New York.

Shaver, S. (1991), '"Considerations of Mere Logic": The Australian Age Pension and the Politics of Means Testing', in Myles, J. and Quadagno, J. (eds), *States, Labor Markets and the Future of Old Age Policy*, Temple University Press: Philadelphia, Pa.

Skocpol, T. (1992), *Protecting Soldiers and Mothers, the Political Origins of Social Policy in the United States*, Harvard University Press: Cambridge, MA.

Skocpol, T. and Ikenberry, J. (1983), 'The Political Formation of the American Welfare State in Historical and Comparative Perspective', *Comparative Social Research*, Vol. 6.

Smeeding, T., Torrey, B. and Rainwater, L. (1993), 'Going to Extremes: an International Perspective on the Economic Status of the U.S. Aged',

Working Paper 87, Luxembourg Income Study, CEPS/INSTEAD: Luxembourg.

Smeeding, T., O'Higgins, M. and Rainwater, L. (1990), *Poverty, Inequality and Income Distribution in Comparative Perspective: The Luxembourg Income Study (LIS)*, The Urban Institute Press: Washington, D.C.

Smeeding, T., Torrey, B. and Rein, M. (1988), 'Levels of Well-being and Poverty Among the Elderly and Children in the US and Other Major Countries', in Palmer, J., Smeeding, T. and Torrey, B. (eds), *The Vulnerable*, The Urban Institute: Washington D.C.

Smith, B. and Townsend, P. (1965), *The Poor and the Poorest*, Bell and Sons: London.

Smith, R. and Wearing, M. (1987), 'Do Australians Want the Welfare State?', *Politics*, Vol. 22.

Smith, R. and Wearing, M. (1990), 'Contemporary Public Opinion and Welfare Policies in Australia, Britain and Sweden', in Saunders, Peter (ed.), *Social Policy in Australia: What Future for the Welfare State*, SPRC Reports and Proceedings No. 80, Social Policy Research Centre, University of New South Wales: Sydney.

Smith, T. (1987), 'That Which We Call Welfare by any Other Name Would Smell Sweeter: An Analysis of the Impact of Question Wording on Response Patterns', *Public Opinion Quarterly*, Vol. 51.

Social Policy Division, Department of Social Security (1993), *Better Incomes for Older Australians?*, Department of Social Security: Canberra.

Stephens, J.D. (1979), *The Transition from Capitalism to Socialism*, Macmillan: London.

Stephens, J.D. (1995), 'The Scandinavian Welfare States, Achievements, Crisis and Prospects', Discussion Paper No. 67, United Nations Research Institute for Social Development: Geneva.

Stephens, J.D., Huber, E. and Ray, L. (forthcoming), 'The Welfare State in Hard Times', in Kitschelt, H., Lange, P., Marks, G. and Stephens, J.D. (eds), *Continuity and Change in Contemporary Capitalism*.

Sussman, B. (1986), 'Do Blacks Approve of Reagan?, It Depends on Who's Asking', *Washington Post*, (weekly edn), 10 February.

Swidler, A. (1986), 'Culture in Action: Symbols and Strategies', *American Sociological Review*, Vol. 51, April.

Taylor-Gooby, P. (1991), *Social Change, Social Welfare and Social Science*, Harvester Wheatsheaf: London.

Taylor-Gooby, P. (1995), 'Comfortable, Marginal and Excluded: Who Should Pay Higher Taxes for a Better Welfare State?', in Jowell, R. et al. (eds), *British Social Attitudes: The 12th Report,* Dartmouth: Aldershot.

Taylor-Gooby, P., George, V. and Bonoli, M.G. (1995), *Squaring the Welfare Circle in Europe, European Welfare Futures,* The Working Papers, Squaring the Welfare Circle Project, University of Kent at Canterbury.

Thane, P. (1982), *Foundations of the Welfare State,* Longman: London.

Therborn, Göran (1980), *The Ideology of Power and the Power of Ideology,* Verso: London.

Titmuss, R.M. (1962), *Income Distribution and Social Change,* George Allen and Unwin: London.

Titmuss, R.M. (1963), 'War and Social Policy', in *Essays on 'The Welfare State',* 2nd edn, Unwin University Books: London.

Titmuss, R. M. (1970), *The Gift Relationship, From Human Blood to Social Policy,* George Allen and Unwin: London.

Titmuss, R. M. (1974), *Social Policy,* George Allen and Unwin: London.

Titmuss, R.M. (1976), *Commitment to Welfare,* 2nd edn, George Allen and Unwin: London.

Tourangeau, R., Rasinski, K., Bradburn, N. and D'Andrade, R. (1989), 'Carryover Effects in Attitude Surveys', *Public Opinion Quarterly,* Vol. 53.

Townsend, P. (1968), 'Introduction: Does Selectivity Mean a Nation Divided?', in *Social Services for All?, Eleven Fabian Essays,* The Fabian Society.

Turner, B. S. (1986), *Citizenship and Capitalism,* Allen and Unwin: London.

Tversky, A. and Kahneman, D. (1982), 'The Framing of Decisions and the Psychology of Choice', in Hogarth, R. (ed.), *Question Framing and Response Consistency,* Jossey-Bass: San Francisco.

United States Department of Health and Human Services (1990), *Social Security Programs Throughout the World - 1989,* Research Report #62, United States Department of Health and Human Services: Washington, D.C.

United States Department of Health and Human Services (1996), *Social Security Programs Throughout the World - 1993,* Research Report #63, United States Department of Health and Human Services: Washington, D.C.

van Parijs, P. (1987), 'A Revolution in Class Theory', *Politics and Society,* Vol. 15, No. 4.

Walker, A. (1991), 'Thatcherism and the New Politics of Old Age', in Myles, J. and Quadagno, J. (eds), *States, Labor Markets and the Future of Old Age Policy,* Temple University Press: Philadelphia, PA.

Walker, A. (ed.) (1996), *The New Generational Contract,* UCL Press: London.

Walsh, A. (1991), 'Low Income Workers and Superannuation', *Labour Movement Strategies for the 21st Century,* Evatt Foundation: Sydney.

Ware, A. and Goodin, R.E. (1990), 'Introduction', in Ware, A. and Goodin, R.E. (eds), *Needs and Welfare,* Sage: London.

Whiteford, P. (1995), *The Use of Replacement Rates in International Comparisons of Benefit Systems,* SPRC Discussion Paper No. 54, Social Policy Research Centre, University of New South Wales: Sydney.

Whiteford, P. and Kennedy, S. (1995), *Incomes and Living Standards of Older People, A Comparative Analysis,* Research Report No. 34, Department of Social Security, HMSO: London.

Whiteford, P., Bradbury, B. and Saunders, P. (1989), 'Poverty Traps in the Australian Social Security System', *Economic Analysis and Policy,* Vol. 19, No. 1.

Wilson, T. and Wilson, D. (1991), 'Issues and Objectives', in Wilson, T. and Wilson, D. (eds), *The State and Social Welfare, The Objectives of Policy,* Longman: London.

Worchel, S. and Cooper, J. (1983), *Understanding Social Psychology,* 3rd edn, Dorsey Press: Homewood, Illinois.

World Bank (1994), *Averting the Old Age Crisis, Policies to Protect the Old* and *Promote Growth,* Oxford University Press: Oxford.

Zaller, J.R. (1992), *The Nature and Origins of Mass Opinion,* Cambridge University Press: Cambridge.

Zapf, W. (1986), 'Development, Structure, and Prospects of the German Social State', in Rose, R. and Shiratori, R. (eds), *The Welfare State East and West,* Oxford University Press: New York.

Zentralarchiv für Empirische Sozialforschung (c.1995), *The International Social Survey Programme: Data and Documentation 1985-1992* (CD-ROM), Universität zu Köln.

Index

Australia
  aged income support system
    14-15, 25-26, 30-31, 38-39, 41,
    107, 112-115, 127
    see also Australia, 'tall
    poppy' means test
  deeming of income 113, 124-
    125, 126-127, 129
  Department of Social Security
    Financial Information Service
    115
  Institute of Actuaries 121
  means testing
    adequacy 111, 127
    complexity 122-123, 128
    financial advice 125-126
    fringe benefits 115, 121-2
    home ownership 114-115,
      115-116, 119-120
    incentives 111, 112, 115-119,
      125, 128, 135
    social justice 111,112, 121,
      127
    stigma 112, 121, 127
    take up 122, 127
    'tall poppy' tests 109-112,
      119, 122, 127, 128, 135

  Strategic Review of the
    Pensions' Income and Assets
    Tests 108-129, 135

Baldwin, P. 10, 12, 23
Barbalet, J. 11-12
benefit generosity 18, 71-72, 76
  n13, 134,142
Bradshaw, J. 28-29

citizens' wage 9
citizenship 7-13, 22, 131, 132
coverage of universal and selective
  transfers 47-49

equivalence scales 45, 54-55, 58-
  60, 74n4

Esping-Andersen, G. 9,12, 22, 26

Flora, P. 22
Friedman, M. 4, 5, 21n2

Germany
  aged income support system 24,
    27-8, 32-33, 39-40
Gini coefficient 67

Hayek, F. v. 4, 5

ideology 78-79, 81
incentives 4, 6, 19
income
  composition of 50-52
  defined 45
income support instruments
  relationship with outcomes 16-17
industrial/achievement model of social policy 9, 10
institutional/redistributive model of social policy 9, 10
insurance model of social policy 10
International Social Survey Programme (ISSP) 23, 77
  methodology 81-82, 83-86

Luxembourg Income Study (LIS) 23, 43, 44, 46, 138-142
  Australian data 46
  German data 46
  methodology 44- 46, 53-55, 56-8, 67
  Swedish data 46

Marshall, T. H. 7-8
means-tested transfers
  distribution of income from 63-65
middle classes, support for social expenditure 6, 12, 22,23, 77-78, 136
Mishra, R. 9
Mitchell, D. 16, 60-61
Myles, J. 9

Norway
  aged income support system 25, 29, 35-6

OECD 1, 31, 73

Pierson, P. 135-137
poverty 5, 18, 132
  defined 53-55
  measures for UK aged 56-58, 75n5
  relationship with selectivity 53-60
poverty traps 4
  see also incentives
public opinion 19
  attitudes of middle classes 92-96
    see also voter support for social expenditure
  party differences 96-99
  state responsibility for incomes of the old 77, 87-91
  support for social role for government 19, 99-104, 134-135
  validity of opinion poll data 79-81, 105

Quadagno, J. 30

redistribution of income 5, 18, 60-70, 133
  relationship with benefit expenditure 18, 68-70, 133
residual model of social policy 9,10

restructuring of welfare state 13-
14,15, 17, 135-137
Ringen, S. 16

Saunders, P. 14-15, 61
selectivity 4, 14-16
   defined 18-19
social assistance 8
social insurance 10,12, 24
social insurance model of social
policy 10
social insurance transfers
   distribution of income from 61-
   63
social integration 3, 19
social rights 7, 9-10, 11, 22
social transfers
   distribution of income from 65
stigma 4, 15
Sweden
   aged income support system 23,
   25, 29, 36-7, 41

take up 4, 19
Titmuss, R. M. 4, 5, 8-9
Townsend, P. 3

United Kingdom
   aged income support system 2-
   5, 23, 24-5, 28-9, 33-34, 40
   Beveridge Report 3, 24
   Child Poverty Action Group 5
   Fabian Socialists 3
   Institute of Economic Affairs 3,
   4

United States
   aged income support system 23,
   26, 30, 37-38, 41
universality 16
   defined 18-19
   relationship with citizenship 11-
   12

universality and selectivity
   debates between 2-7
   in practice 17-18, 46-53
   typology 53

voter support for social
expenditure 6, 15, 17
   see also public opinion

Walker, A. 29
World Bank 1

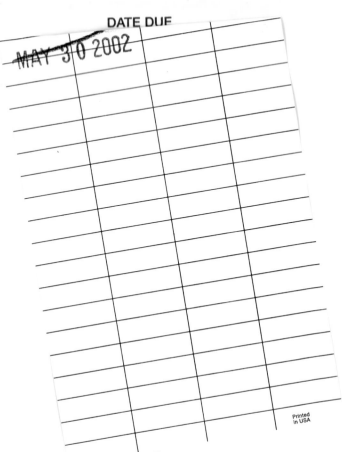

DATE DUE

MAY 3 0 2002

Printed
in USA

HIGHSMITH #45230